# THE SPINE OF SCRIPTURE

## GOD'S KINGDOM FROM EDEN TO ETERNITY

DOMINIC BNONN TENNANT

Published by Information Highwayman
June 2019

*The Spine of Scripture: God's Kingdom from Eden to Eternity*
Version 1.1.0

ISBN 978-0-473-47981-7 (paperback)
ISBN 978-0-473-47982-4 (Kindle)
ISBN 978-0-473-47983-1 (PDF)

Cover design and interior typography by D. Bnonn Tennant. Typography geeks will want to know that the titling typeface is Josefin Sans by Santiago Orozco, the body is set in Andada and Andada SC by Huerta Tipográfica's Carolina Giovagnoli, and footnotes and miscellaneous type are set with IBM Plex Sans (and its condensed variant) by Mike Abbink and Bold Monday.

Unless otherwise indicated, all Scripture translations are original, based on the English Standard Version and Lexham English Bible.

# TABLE OF
# CONTENTS


FOREWORD: *A Note on Language* · · · · · · · · · · · · · · · · · 5

INTRODUCTION: *A Tale of Two Kingdoms* · · · · · · · · · · · 7

CHAPTER 1: *Representation and Rulership* · · · · · · · · · · · 15

CHAPTER 2: *The Divine Council* · · · · · · · · · · · · 33

CHAPTER 3: *What Happened in Eden* · · · · · · · · · · · 49

CHAPTER 4: *A Tale of Two Seeds* · · · · · · · · · · · 65

CHAPTER 5: *When God Began Retaking Adam's Kingdom From Satan* · · · · · 77

CHAPTER 6: *How God is Retaking Adam's Kingdom From Satan* · · · · · 89

CHAPTER 7: *Where We Are Now, and What We Can Look Forward To* · · · · · 105

CHAPTER 8: *The Gospel as a Message of Triumph* · · · · · · · · 115

CHAPTER 9: *The Great Commission as a Directive to Conquer* · · · · · · · · 127

CHAPTER 10: *The Urgency of Preaching Jesus as King of the Western World* · · 143

APPENDIX 1: *But Polytheism! And Other Assorted Concerns* · · · · · · · · 157

APPENDIX 2: *Baptism as a Pledge of Allegiance* · · · · · · · · · · 183

# A NOTE ON LANGUAGE

In my professional field of marketing, there is a phenomenon called marketese. This is the language of marketers: boilerplate jargon that obfuscates the message for the man on the street. You've probably had the misfortune of reading about companies leveraging bleeding edge technical solutions, or impacting performance with innovative best-of-breed strategies.

Thanks to marketese, I have spent over a decade of my professional life becoming increasingly sensitive to the effect of language on clarity. The importance of choosing precisely the right words is always in the forefront of my mind, because it has a measurable effect on revenue.[1] Not having an off-switch for this mindset, I have also made many discoveries in Scripture by wondering how to improve translators' decisions. Over the long term, this has led me to recognize that English Bibles, too, contain boilerplate jargon that obscures the message for the man in the pew. Bibles are full of Christianese.

The importance of this will become evident at points in the chapters that follow, but I mention it in advance because this book is not about my personal trans-

---

1. If this sounds implausible, see for just one random example David Kirkpatrick, "Email Optimization: A single word change results in a 90% lift in sign-ups" on MarketingExperiments (March 2013): https://marketingexperiments.com/email-marketing/email-optimization-a-single-word-change-results-in-a-90-lift-in-sign-ups.

lation philosophy—but it does contain my personal translations, which will be confusing without some explanation. Your reaction to seeing the name Yahweh instead of "the LORD,"[2] or Anointed instead of Christ, or congregation instead of church, will probably be along the lines of, *this guy is a kook.*

I may be a kook; I will let you judge that for yourself. But my whole journey of discovery with kingdom theology has made me acutely aware of how our language shapes our theology—and our blind spots. Dispensing with "Christianese" in favor of straightforward translations has been important for bringing clarity to connections in Scripture which I had been insensitive to—either due to over-familiarity, or to translation choices that obscured them. Therefore, I will typically quote from the LEB or ESV, but with my own translation tweaks. The ESV tends to be decent for overall aesthetics; the LEB for formality. The ESV does not preserve the tetragrammaton; neither preserve words like "man," "fathers," or "sons;" and there are other changes I will make as well without necessarily noting them. In no case am I trying to twist the Scriptures; rather, I am trying to clarify them in English. But if you're ever in doubt, consult the original languages.

2. See D. Bnonn Tennant, "What's the big deal with translating Yahweh as LORD?" (July 2015): https://bnonn.com/whats-the-big-deal-with-translating-yahweh-as-lord/.

INTRODUCTION
# A TALE OF TWO KINGDOMS

*Why do the gospels represent the good news as being about the "kingdom of God"? What is this kingdom, and how does it relate to us today? In this book I trace the surprising narrative of kingdom, from Eden to eternity, that forms the backbone of the Bible—starting by showing that John 3:16 is actually about God transforming man's ruined kingdom into his own perfected one.*

**I**f there is one verse that every Christian knows, it is John 3:16. If there is one verse that summarizes the whole gospel into a single, memorable sentence, it is John 3:16. Yet I am going to start this book by challenging you—because I believe that if there is one verse that most Christians do not understand, it is John 3:16.

> For God loved the world in such a way that he gave his only-begotten son, that whoever believes in him should not perish, but have eternal life (John 3:16).

---

Translations vary as to whether "God so loved," or "this is how God loved." John is deliberately ambiguous here, just as he is in John 1:5 (which, in my view, is best translated, "the darkness has not mastered it"); he picks words with rich ranges of meaning. Translators tend to be uncomfortable with ambiguity, so they try to choose just one meaning for the English text. I think this is a bad translation philosophy, so I am rendering the ambiguity as faithfully as possible by saying, "God loved the world in such a way..."

---

If it turns out that you don't understand John 3:16 as well as you think, and John 3:16 is about the gospel (as everyone agrees), then it will turn out that you don't understand the gospel as well as you think. That's fundamentally the reason I am writing this book. In preparation for preaching on John 3:16, I discovered that it is a focal point for a foundational gospel doctrine I knew nearly nothing about—a doctrine which begins in Genesis, and spans the Bible through to Revelation. The doctrine of kingdom.

This kingdom theology forms the *framework* in which the gospel itself is announced and understood—which is why that gospel is almost ubiquitously called the gospel of the kingdom, or of Jesus, its king.

When I pulled on the thread of kingdom, it turned out, after many years of unraveling, to be more fundamental and more concrete than I had ever suspected. I discovered that kingdom forms the spine of a rich, wild narrative that starts with Adam reigning in Eden, and ends with Jesus reigning in the New Jerusalem—and has lots of surprising twists, characters, and subplots in between.

Nothing I will say here is especially innovative. My own way of explaining it, of course, is my own. Aside from some points of exegesis, I have drawn everything together from the work of other evangelicals—and even my exegesis is not done in a vacuum. Reading this book will take time, and occasionally grit, because I will challenge some ingrained theological traditions. But I speak from both my experience and the testimony of many others when I say that working through this material is unusually enriching and rewarding. For my own part, it has been like discovering a color photo of the Bible after using an old black-and-white snapshot for nearly ten years. Indeed, I believe a clear view of the Bible's kingdom theology is of *foundational* importance to Christianity in the West, for reasons which will become clear in chapters 8–10.

To get into it, then, I am going to begin at the place that was the beginning for me:

## GOD'S LOVE FOR THE WORLD

In preparing to preach on God's love for the world (Gk. *kosmos)*, I discovered a problem. Either I didn't understand what the world was, or I didn't understand what love was.

On the one hand, the Bible describes love as "the bond of perfect unity" (Colossians 3:14). I once heard someone paraphrase this as **onetogetherness,** and I am going to borrow that term because it is so apt. God *is* love (1 John 4:8): three persons fully participating in each other as one being. It is pleasingly pithy to condense this deep doctrine into the simple idea of onetogetherness.[1]

On the other hand, the Bible tells us that the world is very wicked, *hating* Jesus and his followers (John 15:18).

When I plugged onetogetherness into John 3:16 to see how it looked, I discovered that it looked very confusing:

> For God intended onetogetherness with the (wicked) world in such a way that he gave his only-begotten son, that whoever believes in him should not perish, but have eternal life.

How can God intend onetogetherness with the world when the world itself is such an evil thing? Moreover, if God loves it like this, why are we told not to desire

---

onetogetherness with it, or with anything in it? Why are we told that doing so is to *negate* onetogetherness with the Father (1 John 2:15)? Aren't we supposed to imitate our Father? Must we not be perfect, as our Father in heaven is perfect? This seemed contradictory to me: that we must *avoid* onetogetherness with the world, yet God *intends* onetogetherness with the world so much as to send his son to die to save it.

This is the puzzle I faced as I was going to preach on John 3:16. I realized that since I was pretty sure about what love is, my difficulty had to arise from being unclear about what the world itself is. And indeed, if I tried to think of a synonym for world that would make sense of this passage, I couldn't come up with any obvious answer. No wonder I was having trouble when I hadn't figured out what John *meant* when he talked about the world.

The only problem was, none of the commentators I consulted seemed to know either!

A minority of Reformed commentators take the world to be the elect. But this cannot be right because of John's uniform condemnation of the world as wicked. Moreover, under this view, everyone for whom God gave his son will believe, and none will perish, which makes the statement that "whoever" believes virtually incoherent. To say that whoever believes will not perish implies that some will indeed not believe and will therefore perish—which is false if the world is the elect.

Most commentators therefore take the world to be *all people.* They seem to take this for granted, as not even requiring explanation. But this also cannot be right, because we are told *not* to love the world—but certainly we *are* to love all people (Luke 10:25–37). We are told the world hates Jesus—but certainly not *all people* hate Jesus. We are told that God loves the world, and that we ourselves love because he first loved us (1 John 4:19)—

but certainly not all people love him. Most importantly, we are told that Jesus is the savior of the world (1 John 4:14)—but certainly not all people are saved.

How can we understand the world in such a way that it really *is* saved by Jesus?

## WORLD AS KINGDOM

I had to start with the assumption that God *will* save the whole world through Jesus. The *kosmos* will in fact be redeemed. I took this as a foundational fact to inform my understanding of what the world then must be.

Since John 3:16–21 is a commentary on the exchange between Jesus and Nicodemus in John 3:1–15, I began by comparing it to that exchange. What is the key idea there—the idea that Jesus takes up with Nicodemus as soon as he opens his mouth?

It is the kingdom of God.

The whole exchange takes place against the backdrop of God's kingdom.

This helped me to place the eternal life of John 3:16 into context. It is the kingdom of God that will be an eternal kingdom; eternal life belongs to its citizens. When John 3:16 speaks of having eternal life, it is just another way of talking about getting into the kingdom of God (v. 3).

Getting into the kingdom, in turn, is contrasted with perishing in John 3:16—but watch closely; I have nothing up my sleeve: this contrast shows up in verse 16 *because* it is present throughout the first half of John 3. Verse 16 is simply viewing Jesus' words from another angle: believing in the Son to get eternal life is the *same basic idea* as being reborn to see the kingdom of God. They achieve the same goal; they answer the same question.

So if John is contrasting the world with eternal life, and eternal life means entering the kingdom of God, then it follows that John is contrasting the world with the kingdom of God. This comparison naturally invites the conclusion that the *kosmos*, the world, is also a kingdom.

This conclusion is strongly corroborated by John himself, who repeatedly says that the world has a "ruler" (John 12:31; 14:30; 16:11). To have a ruler, it must certainly be a dominion of some kind. So by contrasting the world with the kingdom of God here in John 3, John alerts us that the *kosmos* is his way of referring to the **kingdom of man.**

## SO WHAT IS GOD DOING WHEN HE LOVES THE WORLD?

What he is *not* doing is setting his love on *individual people.* He is setting his love on a kingdom. Let me repeat the passage, including verse 17, and now make the kingdoms there explicit:

> For God intended onetogetherness with the kingdom of man in such a way that he gave his only-begotten son, that whoever believes in him should not perish, but enter the kingdom of God. For God did not send his son into the kingdom of man to condemn it, but in order that the kingdom of man might be saved through him.

When you talk about saving a kingdom, do you mean that every single inhabitant will be saved? When the United States saved England from Germany in the Second World War—to simplify a little!—was no one in England lost?

Of course not. That isn't the point of such language. The point is that the country as a whole was saved from destruction. And that is precisely what John is saying here. The kingdom of man will not be destroyed, but will go on forever. **It will be restored and transformed into an eternal kingdom.**

That might surprise you. After all, isn't the eternal kingdom the kingdom of *God?*

Yes it is. And this begins to solve the puzzle about how God can love the *kosmos* yet instruct us to hate it. We are to hate what it *currently* is, yet God loves what it is *meant* to be—what he made it to be, and what it will one day become again. God intends onetogetherness with the kingdom of man, because the kingdom of man is going to *become* the kingdom of God. John himself describes the end-game this way:

> The kingdom of the world has become the kingdom of our Lord and of his Anointed, and he shall reign forever and ever. (Revelation 11:15)

To boil this down to a simple but provocative statement, here is the bottom line:

If John 3:16 is about the gospel, then the gospel itself is about God saving the kingdom of man.

John 3:16 tells us that God sent his son to redeem the kingdom of man. To make it an eternal kingdom. God is not just on a rescue mission to save individual people. Of course, he *is* going to save individual people—that's in John 3:16 too. The redeemed kingdom of man is made up entirely of individuals who were chosen by the Father, vindicated by the Son, and regenerated by the Spirit. But God isn't saving them just for their sake. His plan is much grander. He is saving an entire kingdom. In fact, he is on a mission not just to rescue people from sin, but to save and restore his own image, in the holy and eternal kingship of the elect, ruled by Jesus. He is going to transform the human kingdom into the heavenly kingdom.

But now we are getting ahead of ourselves. To understand this more fully, we need to turn to Genesis, where man's kingdom got started in the first place.

# CHAPTER 1

# REPRESENTATION AND RULERSHIP

*The kingdom of God and the kingdom of man started out as the same thing, and Adam's representation of God is the paradigm example of how the physical world represents spiritual realities.*

God stands in the divine council;
    he holds judgment in the midst of the gods:
"How long will you judge unjustly
    and lift up the faces of the wicked?
Judge on behalf of the weak and the fatherless;
    vindicate the afflicted and the destitute.
Rescue the helpless and the needy;
    deliver them from the hand of the wicked."
They neither know nor care—
    they stumble in darkness;
    all the foundations of the earth are shaken.
I, I have said, "You are gods,
    sons of the Most High, all of you.
Yet you will die like man,
    and you will fall like any other prince."
Rise up, O God—judge the earth,
    for you shall inherit all the nations. (Psalm 82)

John Piper is one of the few notable evangelicals, at least that I'm aware of, to unambiguously acknowledge what the text of Psalm 82 straightforwardly says:

that God is here "talking to the 'gods,' not to mere humans."[1] Another is Doug Wilson, who makes the same point in his review of *Unseen Realm*:[2]

> Scripture does not teach us that the pagan gods were non-existent. Paul tells us that there were in fact "gods many and lords many" (1 Cor. 8:5–6), and he tells us that genuine demonic forces were involved in idol worship of the pagans (1 Cor. 10:20).[3]

I am encouraged to see evangelical leaders recovering this view, because Psalm 82, accurately read, is a prominent nexus and anchor-point for the biblical theme that undergirds the gospel.

It is a *cosmological* theme—which is to say that it's about the ordering and running of the world. It is a *geographical* theme—which is to say that it's about the territories or domains into which the world is divided. And it is an *evangelical* theme—which is to say that it's about how God is saving a people for himself through the work of the Lord Jesus.

These three ideas—cosmology, geography, and evangelicalism—are drawn together in the Bible into the theme of **kingdom**, since they reflect the three elements required for any kingdom:

1. A king—*who* is doing the ruling?
2. A territory—*where* is he ruling?
3. A people—over *whom* is he ruling?

1. John Piper, "Putting the Gods in Their Place" on Desiring God (1994): http://www.desiringgod.org/articles/putting-the-gods-in-their-place.

2. Michael S. Heiser, *The Unseen Realm: Recovering the Supernatural Worldview of the Bible* (Lexham Press, 2015). Much of what I say in the next few chapters is synthesized from Heiser's work.

3. Douglas Wilson, "Book of the Month/October 2016" on Blog & Mablog (October 2016): https://dougwils.com/s7-engaging-the-culture/book-monthoctober-2016.html.

I've shown from John 3:16 that the gospel is about God's saving the kingdom of man. Now I'd like to expand on this thesis slightly, so we can see how the *features* of kingdom fit together in the gospel. Then I'll spend the rest of this book tracing the threads in Scripture, so we can see the big picture and understand how it works. Here's the thesis:

> The Bible presents the spread of the gospel as God's transforming of Adam's kingdom, ruled by Satan, into his own kingdom, ruled by Jesus. This new kingdom is a spiritual territory of restored human hearts, no longer separated from God by rebellion, but rather annexed from their previous rulers by God himself to dwell and govern there.

With this established, let's set about explaining and proving it.

## THE ORIGINAL KINGS AS THE IMAGE OF GOD

From the creation of man, we have been defined by our kingship over the world. Genesis 1:26–28, the **creation mandate,** couches how we reflect God in terms of kingly activity: rulership or *dominion:*

> Then God said, "Let us make man as our image, as our likeness, and let them have dominion over the fish of the sea and over the birds of the heavens and over the livestock and over all the earth and over every creeping thing that creeps on the earth."

> So God created man as his own image,
>     as the image of God he created him;
>     male and female he created them.

> And God blessed them and God said to them, "Be fruitful and multiply and fill the earth and subdue it, and have dominion over the fish of the sea and over the birds of the heavens and over every living thing that moves on the earth." (Genesis 1:26–28)

That kingship is integral to the image of God becomes especially clear if we abbreviate each instance of dominion given to man in this passage with the word "rule" to emphasize the point:

> And God said, "Let us make man as our image, and let them rule, rule, rule, rule, rule." So God created man as his image, male and female, blessed them and said, "Be fruitful and fill the earth, subdue it, and rule, rule, rule, rule."

The term *redu*, translated "rule" or "have dominion" refers to the power to tread down (*cf.* its use in Joel 3:13); to exercise authority over a given domain (*e.g.*, Leviticus 25:43; Numbers 24:19). In Genesis 1, that domain is the whole world. The imagery of *redu* suggests that God means for Adam to wield the power of pressing order into all creation. By the same token, *kibshu*, typically rendered "subdue" here in Genesis, has military connotations—it actually means to conquer (*e.g.*, Numbers 32:29; 2 Samuel 8:11; 2 Chronicles 28:10, 18). Modern Christians tend to gloss the creation mandate in terms of "stewardship"—and certainly Adam is answerable to God—but the terms Yahweh himself uses here indicate something much stronger: something forceful and vigorous; something not nearly as soft as stewardship, and much more like what is implied in the English term *dominion*. God is not merely making man a custodian in Genesis; he isn't giving him mere supervision of the earth, like a middle-manager. He is making him a king;

giving him free rein over the world. The creation mandate is a **dominion mandate.**

What Adam is given is not *yet* a real kingdom. God does not simply grant him ownership of a pre-built, fully-formed empire. This gift is not so much like a new house as like a construction contract. Adam, following God's example of the first six days, is going to have to decide which raw materials to use, how to tool them, and how to fit them together so as to construct his kingdom. He is going to have to form and to fill. God has not given him a king*dom*, per se, but rather the right and responsibility of king*ship*; now Adam must bend creation to his will in order to take and make the kingdom for God.[4]

That God is *preparing* Adam to rule, rather than simply installing him as a figurehead of a prefabricated domain, is also clear from the presence of the tree of the knowledge of good and evil. Adam is commanded not to eat of this—but the implication is not that he is *never* to eat, but rather that he is not to eat *yet*. It must be in God's time, and not his. This may not seem obvious in Genesis itself, but becomes clear elsewhere in Scripture, where the knowledge of good and evil is presented as judicial wisdom: the paradigmatic skillset of a king (1 Kings 3:7–10; 2 Samuel 14:17; Hebrews 5:14). Such knowledge follows naturally from a king's very job description: rulership requires rightly dividing and ordering; something we have seen God demonstrate already in the wise divisions he made in the world on days one to three, and the order that flowed from these afterward.

---

4. Everything about this suggests that the garden in Eden is an exception to the rest of the world, meant as a model to Adam, rather than just one part of a generally idyllic world. I explore this further in my series on prelapsarian predation: D. Bnonn Tennant, "Prelapsarian predation, part 3: wildness in Genesis 1–2" (September 2015): https://bnonn.com/prelapsarian-predation-3/.

This is why the knowledge of good and evil is something that God himself claims to possess in Genesis 3:22. It is not that this knowledge is bad—it is *good*, it is *god-like* (*cf.* Genesis 3:5), and Adam is made to image God. He will be required to emulate not just God's dominion over the natural world, but also his dominion over the social realm—he will be required to judge in God's stead (*cf.* Exodus 18). He must therefore, at the appointed time, acquire this knowledge, so that he can take up the mantle of command which God made him for. How else can he fulfill his purpose of reflecting and revealing God? If the image of God is kingly, then Adam must eventually gain the knowledge required to exercise kingship. The fact that he was commanded not to take this knowledge for himself does not imply that the knowledge itself was forbidden—rather, it was of such importance that God would only entrust it to him when Adam had first entrusted himself to God. Genesis couches the *imago Dei* in terms of *representative rule*, but it also shows us that the representation has to come before the rule.

Because the image of God is representative, it is also *familial.* In the ancient Near East, where kings commonly claimed to rule on behalf of—or as—gods (a fact that will make far more sense to you as this book progresses), they used the exact phrase "image and likeness" to describe their representative rule and supplicant sonship respectively.[5] Adam is to God as Seth is to Adam—they are made in the likeness of their fathers (Genesis 5:1–3). Adam's rulership and his sonship are inextricably connected, because the very rulership for which he was made is a continuation of the work that

---

5. For a fuller and more nuanced explication, see the excellent primer in chapter 4 of Peter J. Gentry & Stephen J. Wellum, *God's Kingdom through God's Covenants: A Concise Biblical Theology* (Crossway, August 2015).

God had begun: in the six days of creation, God sets an example of what wisely imposing order onto the world looks like, and then creates man to carry this work forward and complete it.

Adam was made to do what he saw the Father doing, what the Father gave him to do. He was made not to seek his own will, but the will of the one who sent him into creation. He was made to bear God's name into the world, revealing and upholding it. This *just is* sonship (*cf.* John 5:19ff; 8:39–44; 17:6)—which is why Luke 3:38 explicitly names him as the son of God.

This is the original biblical cosmology. I am not talking physics here—the word *cosmology* is broader than that. I'm talking about the ordering and running, not just of the natural world, but of the human and also the spiritual world.

Cosmology in the Bible is all about rulership—about who is in charge of whom, and what kinds of judgments they enforce. Do they accurately reveal God's nature as sons, loyally representing him and continuing his work to bring about *shalom*—harmony and peace? Or do they act corruptly in pursuit of their own goals, pressing disorder into the world and shaking the foundations of the earth (Psalm 82:5)?

This being the case, we can make the following important observation to serve as a foundation to build on:

In Eden, God established a kingdom to be ruled by his royal son Adam, with a people who would include all of Adam's descendants, and a territory that would encompass the whole earth.

This was the original kingdom of God—or at least the kernel of it. The entire Bible, one way or another, is concerned with tracing its decline, division, reunion, and eventual restoration.

You probably don't tend to be *looking* for this theme in Scripture, and so you probably don't often notice it. But once you know it's there, and indeed that the Bible presupposes it, you will begin to notice that it's surprisingly important—as I showed with regard to John 3:16. Kingdom theology is right there on the surface of the text, if we only have the framework within which to express it. The narrative trajectory of the Bible begins with God commanding man to build him a kingdom, and ends with God promising to perfect the kingdom that man then went and built for himself instead. The whole arc of Scripture is a story about how Adam's kingdom gets ruined, refused, reclaimed, and finally—after quite a few more refusals and reclaimings—renewed.

But to understand exactly how this works, we need to understand just how extensive the idea of imaging is in the Bible. It is not confined to Adam's rule on God's behalf.

## THE CREATED WORLD AS THE IMAGE OF THE SPIRITUAL

If man images God by representing him, the rest of the world also images spiritual realities in various ways. One God created all things, both visible and invisible, and it is no coincidence that when he becomes incarnate, he has a habit of referring to invisible things by using their visible images. Knowing how the physical world reflects, and is based on, the spiritual realm turns out to be important for understanding a great deal of what Jesus has to say, because he often takes the spiritual meaning of words as their *primary* meaning—in confusing contrast to every other human being ever. A prominent example is food, which to Jesus *first* describes partaking of God through faithful service, assimilating his very nature by the joining of the Spirit— and only *second* refers to ordinary physical eating (John 4:31–35; 6:27–35, 48–58; *cf.* Matthew 16:11–12). Similarly, water means spirit first, and stuff you drink second— *e.g.* John 3:5; 4:10–15; 7:37–39.

This is just a simple illustration for the broader concept I want to focus on: that the physical and spiritual realms are linked in unexpected ways. Water is not merely *like* spirit, but spirit is the *original* water—what mundane water images or represents. Spirit is the archetype of water. In the same way, we see the tabernacle and temple are constructed according to a heavenly archetype revealed to Moses (Exodus 25:9, 40), where the mercy seat images the throne of God, and the cherub statues image (literally) the heavenly throne-guardians (Exodus 37:7–9; 1 Kings 6:23–29; *cf.* Isaiah 6:2; Ezekiel 1:22–28; 1 Kings 22:19). At the peak of creation, man images God, revealing his nature in the physical world. As Bill Mouser has observed, although we think of this as anthropomorphic, we've actually got it backwards; rather, mankind, along with much of creation, is theomorphic.[6]

## IMAGING & GEOGRAPHY

The reason this is important for us is because the same kind of imaging or representation takes place with geography. What happens in spiritual places is linked to what happens in earthly places.

6. William E. & Barbara K. Mouser, *The Story of Sex in Scripture* (International Council for Gender Studies, 2013), loc. 722.

## Deep places

A helpful example of this in the New Testament is the story of Legion and the pigs (Mark 5:1–13; Luke 8:26–33; Matthew 8:28–32). You've probably wondered why Jesus let the demons go into the pigs, and why they then rushed into the sea.[7] The answer would probably have been obvious to an ancient reader, which is why the gospel authors don't explain it: in their world, water was believed to be a natural barrier to spirits. For instance, deceased spirits in ancient lore often had to cross a river, like the Styx, to enter the land of the dead; the water functioned to confine them in their proper domain. Ghosts are even destroyed in some myths by driving them into the sea.

In Luke, Legion begs Jesus not to send him *into* the *abbussou*, "abyss." *Abbusou* is often translated "bottomless pit" and obviously refers to a spiritual place (so Revelation 9:1; 11:7 etc). But it is also the word used in the LXX to translate the "great deep" in places like Genesis 1:2 and 7:11, and refers to the physical sea.

But in Mark's account, by contrast, Legion begs Jesus not to drive him *out of* the *chora*. Most translations render this "country" or "region," but *chora* also simply means the land in opposition to the sea (*cf.* Acts 27:27). Given the seaside location of the encounter, understanding it this way nicely harmonizes Mark with Luke: when Legion says he doesn't want to be driven *out of* the land, he is equally saying that he doesn't want to be driven *into* the sea—the abyss. So he asks to go into the pigs instead.

---

7. Jason Robert Combs, "A Ghost on the Water? Understanding an Absurdity in Mark 6:49–0," JBL 127, no. 2 (2008), 345–58: http://www.michaelsheiser.com/TheNakedBible/MarkGhost.pdf. This connection takes on special significance when we remember that the Jews believed demons to be spirits of deceased nephilim rather than fallen angels.

Why does Jesus allow this? Because he intends to get rid of Legion for good, and letting him go into the pigs gives a convenient physical form to what's going on. His disciples can't see unclean spirits go into the abyss—but they can see unclean beasts go into the sea. So this gives a physical proof of Jesus' power, not just in expelling the demons, but also in dealing permanently to them. The physical events image the spiritual events.

Now, this isn't to say the abyss in the spiritual world is somehow identical with the ocean in the physical world. If it were, then exorcism would be as simple as throwing a demoniac into the water! Indeed, believing that representation is *causal* is the exact idea behind sympathetic magic, idolatry, and certain forms of sacramentalism. The Bible isn't out to draw some kind of "map" of cosmic geography, let alone establish causal connections; rather it *represents* the spiritual realm through the physical world.

*High places*

While the sea represents the abyss where demons are confined, mountains represent a place where earth and heaven meet. They are therefore associated with the presence of gods. (The same is true of trees.) In vast numbers of religions, mountains are where gods reside, or where they presence themselves on earth. The transfiguration of Jesus happened on a mountain—probably Mount Hermon (Matthew 17:1–8, Mark 9:2–8, Luke 9:28–36; 2 Peter 1:16–18). In Ugarit, just to the north of Israel, the high god El was thought to meet in the palace of his vice-regent, Ba'al, on Mount Tsaphon. In Greece, the gods met to hold council on Mount Olympus. In Israel, of course, Yahweh presenced himself first on Mount Horeb or Sinai (Exodus 3:1; 19–31), and later in the temple on Mount Tsiyon (Psalm 9:11; 48:1–2; 74:2;

132:13; Joel 2:1; 3:17). The encounter between Elijah and the 450 priests of Baʿal takes place on Mount Carmel (1 Kings 18). The Samaritans believed God presenced himself on Mount Gerizim (*cf.* John 4:20). Altars were routinely built to pagan gods in high places (Deuteronomy 12:2; 1 Kings 12:31–32); and these could include artificial mountains that functioned as stairways to heaven (*e.g.* 2 Kings 17:9; *cf.* Genesis 28:12; John 1:51)—this is the idea behind ziggurats,[8] which is what the Tower of Babel would have been given its location and time period (*cf.* Genesis 11:1–9).[9]

*Sacred space*

The presence of deity was important to the ancient worldview in another way, which returns us to the concept of kingdom: there was a territorial aspect to it. We see how this cashes out with the story of Naaman in 2 Kings 5. In verse 17, Naaman says:

> ...please let a load of soil on a pair of mules be given to your servants, for your servant will never again bring a burnt offering and sacrifice to other gods, but only to Yahweh (2 Kings 5:17).

Understanding why Naaman does this gets us to a key concept in understanding the kingdom of God itself. What's happening here is fundamentally the same as what's happening in Exodus 3:5 and Joshua 5:15, where God tells Moses and Joshua to take off their sandals because they are standing on holy ground. It is fundamen-

---

8. See for example "What Was the Importance of Ziggurats in Ancient Mesopotamia?" on DailyHistory.org: https://dailyhistory.org/What_Was_the_Importance_of_Ziggurats_in_Ancient_Mesopotamia.

9. John H. Walton, "Is there Archaeological Evidence for the Tower of Babel?" on Associates for Biblical Research (May 2008): http://www.biblearchaeology.org/post/2008/05/Is-there-Archaeological-Evidence-for-the-Tower-of-Babel.aspx.

tally the same as what's happening in Exodus 19, when the Lord says to Moses,

> Go to the people and consecrate them today and tomorrow, and let them wash their garments and be ready for the third day. For on the third day Yahweh will come down on Mount Sinai in the sight of all the people. And you shall set limits for the people all around, saying, "Take care not to go up into the mountain or touch the edge of it. Whoever touches the mountain shall be put to death. No hand shall touch him, but he shall be stoned or shot; whether beast or man, he shall not live." When the trumpet sounds a long blast, they shall come up to the mountain. (Exodus 19:10–13)

It is fundamentally the same thing that is happening in the threefold structure of the temple: the courtyard, the holy place, and the holy-holy place. And it is also fundamentally the same thing that is happening with Israel's laws about ritual cleanness, and restoring that cleanness when a member of the covenant community became ritually impure or defiled.

Certain space is *sacred*. It is set apart by and for the presence of God. The land of Israel was sacred, because it was God's land—he dwelt there, in the temple in Jerusalem. It was his living-space, which he graciously shared with his people. So in order to live in the land, you yourself had to be set apart for God by observing the ritual purity laws. The closer you got to God, the more sacred the ground was. The twice-holy place in the temple, the holy of holies, was so sacred that only one man could enter once per year. Although there was no necessary *ontological* difference between sacred and ordinary space, or ritually clean and unclean people— *i.e.*, they did not differ in nature or essence—there was a *covenantal* difference which had serious ramifications for anyone involved.

---

Ontology was not *irrelevant*: sacred space was where God presenced himself, and ritual purity was enacted in the body. But neither was ontology in itself the issue; there is a significant difference between *representation* and *essence*. God does not by nature have physical form, so we have to say that the *shekhinah* was in some sense ontologically distinct from him; and similarly, performing certain rituals in the body does not effect an essential change that makes one more "compatible" with God's presence. I mention this here because it is one end of a thread which terminates in the incarnation, where the separation between representation and essence actually does get broken down—as I'll touch on in chapter 6.

---

Naaman knew that Israel was sacred to Yahweh. So he asked for enough dirt to make a mini-Israel in Syria—a small space set aside for Israel's God, where he could be worshiped. A modern analogy would be an embassy on foreign soil. In a similar but opposite way, the priests of Dagon refused to step on the threshold of their own temple after Yahweh so conspicuously seized it from their god in 1 Samuel 5:4–5; they didn't want to risk entering space owned by an enemy deity.

## WHERE COSMOLOGY AND GEOGRAPHY INTERSECT

When we put cosmology and geography together, we start moving in a straight line toward the gospel. This is because the intersection between cosmology and geography is *kingdom*. Cosmology is about the order and running of the world. *Who* is ruling? Geography is about the division and features of the world. *Where* are they are ruling? (We'll get to the question of the people *over whom* they are ruling in due course.)

Now that we have a basic grasp of how these elements fit into the Bible, we are faced with a rather intriguing question:

If Israel was the sacred space of Yahweh—if Israel, in other words, was the part of the world ordered and run by the God of the Bible—then...what about the *rest* of the world?

To start answering this, let's go back to John. I've noted that John views the world, the *kosmos*, not just as humanity in general, but as a kingdom. He explicitly calls it such in Revelation 11:15, and he refers to **"the ruler of this world"** three times in his gospel (John 12:31; 14:30; 16:11).

I don't think it is too difficult to work out who the ruler of this world is. For one thing, John himself elsewhere states that "the whole world lies in the power of the evil one" (1 John 5:19). For another, in Luke 4, we learn that just before Jesus began his ministry,

> the devil took him up and showed him all the kingdoms of the world in a moment of time, and said to him, "To you I will give all this authority and their glory, for it has been delivered to me, and I give it to whom I will. If you, then, will worship me, it will all be yours." (Luke 4:5–7; par. Matthew 4:8–9)

We see here in very clear terms that the world, the dominion of man, is divided into smaller kingdoms—and that the whole lot has been handed over to Satan. Some people think he is lying on this point—he is, after all, the father of lies. But that doesn't make sense *here*, because Jesus could not be tempted by a deal that Satan could not make good on. Satan is offering to let Jesus short-circuit the process of becoming the king over the world, just as he originally did with Adam. In this case, he tempts Jesus with a quick win, where he *legitimately* gets kingship from Satan without a fight—but the catch is that Satan gets the moral victory. If Satan had no legitimate claim to the kingdoms of the world, there would be no *temptation* here.

Now, this isn't to say that Satan controls everything single-handedly. Just as human kingdoms are organized with a hierarchy of other rulers beneath the king, so Satan's kingdom is organized similarly. There are individual spiritual rulers who control specific nations, as the Bible shows in several places:

1. **In Daniel 10** we learn of the prince or ruler of Persia (v. 13), and the prince of Greece (v. 20): these are spiritual beings who are engaged in battle with the spiritual being who visits Daniel—and with Michael, the prince of Israel (Daniel 10:13, 21; 12:1).[10]

2. **In Ephesians 6:12** we learn that we ourselves are engaged in this battle, not against flesh and blood, but against the "rulers, against the authorities, against the cosmic powers over this present darkness, against the spiritual forces of evil in the heavenly places" (*cf.* Ephesians 3:10).

3. **In Psalm 82** as we've seen, there is a whole assembly of these spiritual rulers whom God calls to account.

4. **In 1 Corinthians 2:8** Paul observes that "none of the rulers of this age understood" God's hidden plan of salvation through the gospel—"for if they had, they would not have crucified the Lord of glory."[11]

10. The identification of Michael as the prince of Israel is suggestive, given that Yahweh is the ruler of Israel; possibly Michael is the proper name of the angel of Yahweh who appears many times in the Old Testament. Ultimately this is of little importance, but it is intriguing. I have yet to follow this thread to its conclusion, but for a primer on the divine nature of the angel of Yahweh, see D. Bnonn Tennant, "Overt Christology in the Old Testament, part 2: the angel of Yahweh" (November 2015): https://bnonn.com/overt-christology-in-the-old-testament-2/.

11. See "Why think the rulers of 1 Corinthians 2:6–8 are gods?" in Appendix 1.

These beings are so much in charge of the human world that Paul can speak as if *they themselves* crucified Jesus. But Satan has authority over them all. Geographically, all the lands of the earth are his. Cosmologically, he is ruling, he is calling the shots. The world is his kingdom. Hence Paul, in 2 Corinthians 4:4, calls him the *god of this world/age* (*cf.* Galatians 1:4; Luke 8:12).

---

On 2 Corinthians 4:4, some commentators demur, interpreting Yahweh as the god of this age; *e.g.,* Donald Hartley argues that there are no semantic parallels for Satan as a god in Paul's thinking, and that he is instead drawing on Isaiah 6:9–10 where Yahweh is the active agent.[12] But this supposes that *semantic* parallels are the only kind that matter, which obviously commits the word-concept fallacy. If we expand our search to *conceptual* parallels, there is an abundance of material that Paul could be drawing on. Hartley's word-concept error manifests in several ways: (i) Claiming that there is no precedent for calling Satan the god of this world, when in fact Psalm 82 is excellent precedent when combined with Ephesians 2:2, where Paul is plainly speaking of Satan as the ruler of all spiritual powers; (ii) Discounting the instrumental role in salvific blindness explicitly attributed to Satan by Jesus in Luke 8:12 (par. Mark 4:15; Matthew 13:19) and strongly implied by Paul in Ephesians 2:2; (iii) Ignoring the relationship between moral depravity and intellectual inability, and thus the connotations of Satan's power as described in places like 1 John 5:19. Given these factors, along with the awkwardness of taking Yahweh as the god of this age when Satan fits the label so aptly and straightforwardly, I stand by the majority of modern exegetes on this point. That said, my case in no way rides on this; very little changes if I am wrong.

---

The sacred space of Israel was the sole exception—God dwelt there and he was in charge. You can probably see how this lends a great deal of import to the first two commandments, and the problem of idolatry: to worship other gods was to effectively overturn Israel's status as sacred space by rededicating the land to beings who didn't own it. Hence the punishment of exile. I won't pursue that issue further here, since we live on the other side of the cross; the point I rather want to make is that ever since Jesus said, "It is finished," and the curtain of the temple was torn in two—and actually,

12. Donald E. Hartley, 2 Corinthians 4:4: "A Case for Yahweh as the 'God of this Age'," *The 57th Annual Meeting of the Evangelical Theological Society* (November 2005): https://rdtwot.files.wordpress.com/2007/10/2cor-44.pdf.

since at least the exile—God has not dwelled in Israel. The covenant that made the land and the people his was abrogated (Hebrews 8:13).

So, does that mean that there's now no longer *any* part of the world that isn't Satan's?

Yes...and no.

Yes in the sense that, if a kingdom is a human kingdom, it is in Satan's sights, and may be under a great deal of his control.

But no in the sense that God is doing something about this. He is taking back Satan's territory for himself since the cross, where he "disarmed these rulers and authorities and put them to open shame, by triumphing over them in it" (Colossians 2:15; *cf.* Ephesians 1:21).

To understand how this works, we first need to understand who Satan and his cronies are, and how they came to be in charge of Adam's kingdom in the first place.

# CHAPTER 2

# THE DIVINE COUNCIL

*Israel, like all ancient Near Eastern peoples, conceived of the world as governed by a cosmic dynasty or household bureaucracy—a bureaucracy the Bible calls the divine council. Prophets were brought into this council when they were commissioned.*

How did Adam's kingdom get given to Satan? To understand this, we need to start by asking how both characters fit into the biblical cosmology to begin with.

The Bible does not explicitly lay out every detail of this for us; hence we can easily miss it—even though the whole arc of redemptive history takes it for granted. It is within the story of the ups and downs of God's dynasty that each part of the Bible is written. This story is implicit, presupposed—but there are enough clues across the Bible that we can easily trace the broad strokes when we know what to look for. I will only cover the most important elements here; there are many others that will probably start to emerge in your own reading, as you become more fluent with the patterns that Scripture uses to develop this narrative.

## RULERSHIP IN THE SPIRITUAL PLACES

To understand how Satan and these other spiritual beings came to be in charge, we first need to understand the overarching cosmology of the Bible. We've seen that the kingdom on earth was originally given to Adam. But while he was the first *human* ruler, he was created to fit into a larger council that included *spiritual* beings. This is where things get quite strange to our secularized, Western sensibilities, because we discover that the spirit world of the Bible is not as sanitized as we like to imagine.

To see this, we only need to know certain religious terms that had particular significance for the original audience of the Bible; a significance that is not obvious to us, because we are so far removed from their thought-world, their zeitgeist. These terms are what you might call religious memes, rather like *lamb of God* is a kind of meme for us. By *meme* I don't mean a picture with a silly caption, but a unit of cultural information, or an idea that everyone within a certain group is familiar with. There are "codewords" in every language and culture that represent religious concepts—as *lamb of God* does to Christians—that no one expects an explanation for; they are just part of the natural religious language of that culture.

This was true of ancient Jews and other Semitic peoples, just as much as of modern Christians. And if we don't know their memes or codewords, we miss a lot of the messaging in the Bible—just as someone today would miss a lot if he didn't know about the Passover when he heard that Jesus is the lamb of God.

The memes of the Hebrew Bible were not always exclusive to Israel—indeed, because the Bible was written in the *general* language of its time, much of the particular religious vocabulary within that language came along for the ride. This vocabulary was shared to varying degrees with the surrounding nations, and especially with Ugarit (part of Canaan) to the north, because Ugaritic and Hebrew were cognates: they had a common ancestor, and thus many commonalities, much like German and Dutch, or Spanish and Italian.

The Bible does not use these memes in a *pagan* way, like Israel's neighbors did. But it does take the vocabulary and adapt it to the biblical worldview. If we want to decipher the overarching biblical cosmology, we therefore need to know this vocabulary. We need to be on the lookout for certain codewords.

## ANCIENT NEAR EASTERN RELIGIOUS MEMES

The overarching meme which these codewords describe is typically called the *divine council*. This was a kind of cosmic household that functioned as a ruling bureaucracy: a group of deities, led by a high god, who together were in charge of administering the cosmos and deciding what happened on earth. With some variations, this divine assembly appeared in all Mediterranean and ANE religions; it was a standard feature of their cosmologies.[1] The gods of the divine council were typically referred to as:

- **Gods.** Obviously.

- **Sons of God.** This is a very common term, illustrating the *dynastic* nature of the divine assembly as a ruling household—a family of gods under a supreme father-figure.

1. For both scholarly and lay-level introductions to the divine council from a broadly evangelical perspective, see Michael Heiser's website, http://www.thedivinecouncil.com/.

- **God's council/divine council/assembly of the gods.** Whereas "sons of God" speaks of the family nature of the assembly, the word "council" gets to the heart of its bureaucratic, cosmological function in governing the world.

- **Holy assembly/council of holy ones.** Gods are set apart from the world of man and are generally unapproachable by us, which is what holiness means.

- **Stars of heaven/morning stars.** The idea that stars were divine, or represented divine beings, was a common motif in the ancient world because they were luminous and moved of their own accord; morning stars, of course, were the most luminous—thus the most important.

Now, gods don't meet just anywhere. There has to be a special place for them to hold council. And there was a clear commonality with regards to the kind of place they would gather to decide the fates of people and nations:

- **In a lush garden.** This spoke of opulence and beauty, especially in the arid Near East.

- **On a holy mountain.** This should come as no surprise given what we've already seen about the association between deities and mountains or high places, where heaven meets earth.

- **At the source of rivers.** A plentifully-watered place again spoke to the abundance and luxury that only deities, and their kingly representatives on earth, could afford; and in the Bible this also images the life-giving Spirit of God.

- **In the heights of the north.** This is a particular Ugaritic term for the meeting place of Ba'al, which crops up in the Bible for polemical reasons—the term *north* in Hebrew and Ugaritic is *tsaphon,* which was also the name of the mountain of the supreme god, El.

- **In a location adorned with precious stones and paved with sapphire.** Naturally, gods will have only the best accommodation as befits their royal station.

- **Where the supreme god's throne was.** Just as human kings would hold council in their throne-rooms, so divine kings would do the same.

The point I'm getting at, of course, is that all of these terms are common both in ancient Near Eastern *pagan* religions, *and* in the Bible. That might sound disturbing, but it shouldn't be. After all, what are the chances that pagan cultures all came up with the same religious ideas out of whole cloth? Isn't it more probable that they are perversions of actual spiritual realities? And if they are, then certainly the Bible can use the same language to describe those spiritual realities, and correct the parts that pagans distorted.

Let's now work through some of the places where these terms or concepts appear in the Bible, so we can see what the actual spiritual realities are. This will prepare us to understand how they relate to Adam's kingdom.

## GOD'S FIRST DYNASTY: THE DIVINE COUNCIL IN THE BIBLE

We saw at the beginning of chapter 1 that these beings are called **gods,** in Psalm 82:1, 6.[2] Those verses also point us to other key terms. In verse 6, we see indirectly that the persons in question are **sons of God**: "I have said you are gods, sons of the Most High." And in verse 1 we see God standing in the **divine council.** The Hebrew here, *adat el,* is a direct cognate of Ugaritic *'dt 'ilm*—the council of El in Canaanite mythology. Obviously there is a polemical slant, since God is *judging* the gods—but it only functions if the basic premise is the same: that the cosmos is administered by a divine bureaucracy.

That the context of Psalm 82 is rulership should be obvious given the content: the gods are taken to task for judging unjustly and showing partiality; the task of rulers, as I mentioned in discussing Adam's kingship, was to judge justly and impartially (Deuteronomy 1:16–17). These gods have failed to give justice to the weak and the fatherless; rulers were to protect orphans and widows from oppression (Jeremiah 22:2–3). They have not rescued the weak from the hand of the wicked; rulers were to deliver the one who had been seized from the hand of the oppressor (*ibid.*)

The same cosmic bureaucracy is plainly in view in Psalm 89:5–7, which speaks of the **assembly/council of the holy ones.** The Hebrew terms are different here

2. I have taken for granted during the course of this book that the exegesis of Psalm 82 is straightforward, and that elohim, "gods," refers to spiritual beings and not to men. This is because the exegesis is straightforward—provided you can overcome the conditioning of our own religious vocabulary, which automatically connects the Hebrew vocabulary to polytheism or henotheism, and therefore compels us to impute some other meaning to the text. I am sensitive, however, that this talk of other gods is a genuine issue for people who have not encountered such ideas before; so for a detailed interaction with these challenges—including a demonstration that this view of Psalm 82 is the only one that makes sense logically and exegetically—see Appendix 1.

(*qhal/sod qedoshim*), but the concept is obviously the same—especially since we see in Psalm 89:6 that they are composed of the **sons of God** (Hebrew *beney elim*, cognate with Ugaritic *bn 'ilm*). This is a stock motif for divine beings that parallels "sons of the most high" (*beney elyon*) in Psalm 82:6 (*cf.* Psalm 29:1). That Psalm 89:5–7 is a parallel to the council of Psalm 82 cannot be seriously doubted on pain of special pleading—and quite obviously it is not a human council, since human councils do not meet in the skies (89:6); nor is there a single human council in charge of all the nations over the whole earth (Psalm 82:5, 8).

In Job 1:6–12, we see the **sons of God** presenting themselves to Yahweh, and there is a kind of courtroom motif to the scene with a prosecutor character—in Hebrew, the *satan*. This is, no doubt, Satan, but it is incorrect to translate *ha'satan* as a proper name in this case; it literally means the opposer or the accuser.[3] The question of Job's loyalty is raised, an argument is given, and resolutions are made—exactly what we should expect in a meeting of the divine council, since its function was to raise issues, debate them, and come to resolutions about them. This happens again in Job 2:1–6.

We also find the divine council in Micah's vision:

I saw Yahweh **sitting on his throne** with all the armies of heaven standing beside him from his right hand and from his left. And Yahweh said, "Who will entice Ahab so that he will go up and fall at Ramot-Gilead?" Then this one was saying one thing and the other was saying another. Then a spirit came out and stood before Yahweh and said, "I will entice him," and Yahweh said to him, "How?" He said, "I will go out and I will be a false spirit in the mouth of all his prophets." And he

3. D. Bnonn Tennant, "Constructive criticism of The Unseen Realm #2: who is ha'satan?" (October 2015): https://bnonn.com/constructive-criticism-of-the-unseen-realm-2/.

> said, "You shall entice and succeed, go out and do so."
> (1 Kings 22:19–22; par. 2 Chronicles 18:18–22; *cf.* Daniel
> 4:17)

The setting is a throneroom or a palace; Yahweh is on his throne and there is a heavenly host around him. Again an issue is raised—how to bring about Ahab's demise—and this time the whole council is involved in the debate. Finally, one solution is accepted by God. The issue is raised, debated, and resolved.

The characters present are here described as the heavenly host—God's army. It isn't completely clear whether each and every one is involved in the council; we learn in another divine council scene, Daniel 7, that the heavenly host is beyond reckoning (Daniel 7:10; *cf.* Psalm 68:17; Hebrews 12:22; Revelation 5:11)—but since spiritual beings need not be constrained by the physical logistics of debate, there's no clear reason to doubt the involvement of each member. The Bible doesn't explicitly state whether every member of the heavenly host is also a member of the divine family; and, if so, whether they are all members of the council; and, if so, what the hierarchy looks like. We do know that there are archangels—literally "power angels," but more helpfully translated "angels in charge"—but we don't know if they are in charge by merit of greater ontological power, by closer familial connection, by mere merit of assignment, or some combination thereof. The descriptions of Satan that we'll look at in the next chapter perhaps suggest that some angels are ontologically superior to others, but I am very reluctant to push the imagery too far. All we can say for sure is that the beings designated the "sons of God" are also called archangels, and they have greater authority than the heavenly host in general. This is *broadly* in line with Ugaritic religion, in which there were two tiers of gods: the sons of El, who ruled certain districts and provinces, and a larger group of lesser gods who acted as messengers and warriors. But how close the correlation is I am not sure.

## PROPHETS AS MEMBERS OF THE DIVINE COUNCIL

The passages above are the most obvious divine council "sightings," but they are far from the only ones. We also see a very similar motif in the commissioning of prophets, and this moves us toward our goal of understanding how Adam and Satan fit into the biblical cosmology:

> In the year of the death of Uziyahu the king, I saw **the Lord sitting on a high and raised throne,** and the hem of his robe was filling the temple. Seraphs were standing above him, each with six wings; with two he covered his face, with two he covered his genitals, and with two he flew. And the one called to the other and said, "Holy, holy, holy is Yahweh of armies! His glory fills the whole earth!" And the pivots of the thresholds shook from the sound of those who called, and the temple was filled with smoke.
>
> And I said, "Aiee to me; I am destroyed—for I am a man of unclean lips, and I am living among a people of unclean lips, and my eyes have seen the king, Yahweh of armies!" Then one of the seraphs flew to me, and in his hand was a hot coal he had taken from the altar with tongs. And he touched my mouth, and he said, "Look! This has touched your lips and has removed your guilt, and your sin is annulled."
>
> Then I heard the voice of the Lord saying, "Whom shall I send? And who will go for us?" And I said, "I am here! Send me!" And he said, "Go and say this to my people..." (Isaiah 6:1–8)

Notice again the divine council elements. The setting is God's throne-room with seraphs present (later we'll see that Satan is a seraph). An issue is raised, as indicated by the plural language, "who will go for *us?*" Isaiah volunteers and the issue is resolved by commissioning him.

Here's another example of prophetic commissioning where it is not so obvious:

> And the Word of Yahweh came to me, saying, "Before I formed you in the womb I knew you, and before you came out from the womb I consecrated you; I appointed you as a prophet to the nations."
>
> Then I said, "Ah, Lord Yahweh! Look, I do not know how to speak, for I am a youth." But Yahweh said to me, "You must not say, 'I am a youth,' for to whomever I send you, you will go, and whatever I command you, you will speak. Do not be afraid of them, for I am with you to deliver you," declares Yahweh. Then Yahweh stretched out his hand and he touched my mouth, and he said to me, "Look, I have put my words in your mouth." (Jeremiah 1:4–9)

Now, this *doesn't* look like divine council imagery, but there are clues here that we can piece together by looking elsewhere in Jeremiah. The first thing to notice is that the Word of Yahweh is a *physical presence* whom Jeremiah addresses *as* Yahweh. The Word comes to him, not as a voice in his ear like we tend to assume, but as a person who touches Jeremiah, and to whom Jeremiah speaks, addressing him as Yahweh himself. The same kind of thing happens with Abram in Genesis 15:1–5: the Word comes to him in a vision, so he can see it (v. 1), and takes him outside (v. 5). It happens again in 1 Samuel 3: the Word of Yahweh is said to come in visions (v. 1), and stands near Samuel's bed (v. 10); and in verse 21 we read that, "Yahweh *appeared* again at Shiloh, for Yahweh revealed himself to Samuel at Shiloh by the Word of Yahweh."

When we pay close attention, it is obvious that the Word, and Yahweh, are the same person; and this person appears in embodied form. We should expect this given John 1:1—"In the beginning was the Word, and the Word was with God, and the Word was God." John gets his theology from the Hebrew scriptures.[4]

In case you're wondering what all this has to do with the divine council, let's now look at chapter 23 of Jeremiah:

> Thus says Yahweh of armies, "You must not listen to the words of the prophets who prophesy to you. They are deluding you with visions of their mind, they do not speak from the mouth of Yahweh. They are continually saying to those who disregard the Word of Yahweh, 'Peace it will be to you,' and to each one who walks in the stubbornness of his heart they say, 'Calamity will not come upon you.' **For who has stood in the council of Yahweh, that he has seen and heard his Word?** Who has listened attentively to his Word and heard it?" (Jeremiah 23:16–18)

We find here—quite explicitly if you don't just skip over the language—that prophets are commissioned by God when they stand in his council and see his Word. The Word of Yahweh stands with them in the council of Yahweh.

Put another way, when the Word comes to prophets, they are brought into the royal courtroom, amidst the divine council. This isn't always stated explicitly, but turns out to have happened "behind the scenes," as comparing Jeremiah 1 and 23 illustrates. Given the Hebrew penchant for omitting details that were taken for granted, it's a safe bet that *any* time God reveals himself

---

4. For a fuller exploration of the various ways that the Son appears quite overtly in the Old Testament, see D. Bnonn Tennant, "Overt Christology in the Old Testament" (November 2015): https://bnonn.com/overt-christology-in-the-old-testament.

to man, his divine council is with him. That's just the way the whole process works.

Lest this seem like too sweeping a bet to make on the basis of such limited evidence, consider another example: did you know that the divine council was involved in the giving of the law to Moses? If my bet is correct, we should expect it, since Moses was a prophet—*the* prophet. But it certainly isn't stated in Exodus, is it?

Indeed not; in Exodus we have only a *hint* that the divine council is present:

> And Moses and Aaron, Nadab and Abihu, and seventy from the elders of Israel went up [Mount Sinai]. And they saw the God of Israel, and what was under his feet was like **sapphire tile work** and like the very heavens for clearness. And toward the leaders of the Israelites he did not stretch out his hand, and they beheld God, and they ate, and they drank. (Exodus 24:9–11)

Notice the interesting detail about what is under God's feet in this vexingly brief glimpse of a physical encounter with Yahweh: something like sapphire tile work. This is another hallmark of the meeting place of the divine council; Ba'al's palace was paved with sapphire; so this *suggests* that the divine council is nearby. It is not explicitly said—but knowing how Hebrew high-context discourse leaves out details that readers would take for granted, we can reasonably predict it. And this is exactly what we find in Deuteronomy 33:2, which explicitly recollects the giving of the law at Sinai:

> Yahweh came from Sinai,
> and he dawned upon them from Seir;
> he shone forth from Mount Paran,
> and he came with myriads of **holy ones,**

at his right hand a fiery law for them. (Deuteronomy 33:2, LEB)[5]

Who are the holy ones? Well, Psalm 89:5 describes them
as a council. This is why Paul says in Galatians 3:19 that
the law was "put in place through angels," and Stephen
says in Acts 7:53 that the Jews "received the law as delivered by angels," and Hebrews 2:2 says it was a "message
declared by angels." It was just taken for granted by the
Jews—so obvious as to not require stating.

In the same way, it was taken as obvious that a
prophet was someone who had been brought into God's
presence, had seen the Word of Yahweh, and had by
implication participated in the divine council. This is,
according to Jeremiah 23:22, the *defining feature* of
prophetic calling. How do you know if someone is a
true prophet, continuing the office of Moses? By
whether he has been in the presence of the Word of
Yahweh. And where the Word was, so was his divine
council.

The situation changes slightly with the New Testament prophets—the apostles—because they lived in the
presence of the *incarnate* Word, who by nature did *not*
have his angelic council present (*cf.* Luke 4:9–11). Yet
they nonetheless were commissioned by him, and this
is why even in the case of Saul, he is inducted into the
apostolic ranks through a vision of Jesus (Acts 9:3–6).

Ezekiel has an even more impressive encounter
with Yahweh in the divine court, which in that instance
is a kind of "mobile throneroom." Again there are seraphs around the throne—this time called cherubs;
throne-guardians (Ezekiel 1:4–15)—and again there is

5. The Hebrew is a little tricky here, especially in regards to whether Yahweh is coming
from or with the holy ones, and what exactly the fiery law is; compare the LXX's reading, "The Lord is come from Sina, and has appeared from Seir to us, and has hasted
out of the mount of Pharan, with the ten thousands of Cades; on his right hand his angels with him."

the element of sapphire (Ezekiel 1:26). That seraphs and cherubs are basically the same creatures should be clear from Revelation 4:6–9, where the living creatures before the throne are obviously a composite of the seraphs in Isaiah 6:1–4 and the cherubs in Ezekiel 1 and 10. This will become clearer in the next chapter, when we see that Satan is described as both a seraph and a cherub.

There are more subtle examples which further link prophetic calling with being in the presence of God. For instance, according to Hebrew tradition, Enoch was a major prophet; Jude 1:14 refers to him prophesying. Why did the Jews think this, given that none of his prophecies are recorded in Scripture? Genesis 5 gives us a clue:

> When Enoch had lived sixty-five years, he fathered Methusalah. And Enoch **walked with God** after he fathered Methusalah three hundred years, and fathered other sons and daughters. And all the days of Enoch were three hundred and sixty-five years. And Enoch **walked with God, and he was no more, for God took him.** (Genesis 5:21–24)

Now, we have an idiom—a meme even—in the modern Western church. We talk about our "Christian walk;" thus, when we read the expression "Enoch walked with God," we import this meme into it and interpret it as, "Enoch lived in a godly way." But that isn't what it means *absent* this Western expression—as becomes obvious if we switch the characters in the phrase:

Peter walked with Jesus.

What do you imagine now? You see, Enoch was a prophet because he walked in the physical presence of

God, and was, it seems, taken up physically into heaven by God (*cf.* Hebrews 11:5).

This leads us finally to Adam, because we know that he, too, lived in the physical presence of God. Genesis 3:8 says that he "heard the sound of Yahweh God **walking** in the garden in the cool of the day." In fact, the Bible explicitly calls Adam out as the first human member of the divine council—moreover, it does so in a way that clarifies what happened in Eden, and how everything went, as it were, to hell.

# CHAPTER 3
# WHAT HAPPENED IN EDEN

*Adam was created as the first human member of the divine council. The serpent was a shining, serpentine being who didn't like Adam being given dominion of the earth instead of someone higher up…like him.*

We're now ready to see how Adam was the first human member of the divine council—and what he and Satan had to do with each other. This brings us to Eden; to God's original kingdom. The Bible has more to say about what happened in Eden than just what we read in early Genesis. Indeed, in the process of following the clues, we'll make a great deal more sense of early Genesis as well.

## EDEN AS THE DIVINE COUNCIL CHAMBERS

Let us begin with Eliphaz. In his diatribe against Job, he puts the following question to him:

> Are you the first man who was born?
> > Or were you brought forth before the hills?
> **Have you listened in the council of God?**
> > And do you limit wisdom to yourself? (Job 15:7–8)

Eliphaz is obviously referring poetically to Adam—the "first man"—and his rhetorical contrast requires us to understand that while Job had *not* listened in the council of God, Adam *had*. While Eliphaz is not always to be trusted, this does give us a clue to follow, so let's see where it leads. Assuming that Adam listened in the council of God, this would bring some clarity to passages which have historically been puzzling.

If Adam was a human member of the divine council—or at least the first man to have access to it—and if he encountered God in the garden of Eden, and if, as we've seen, the rest of the council's presence is taken as given in such situations; then the garden itself would have been the council meeting-place. Although we never see a throne-room in Eden, this idea is corroborated in at least three other ways:

1. **A garden.** Most obviously, the divine council in ancient Near Eastern religious thought would meet in a garden—which is what Adam was created in.

2. **Rivers.** In Genesis 2, we learn that Eden was the source of four rivers. If you recall the codewords I listed in the previous chapter, this was another common motif for divine council meeting places; in Ugarit, El's council met in a garden at the source of two rivers.

3. **A holy mountain.** The garden meeting-place of El was also held to be on a holy mountain; and the Bible explicitly names Eden as such:

> And the Word of Yahweh came to me, saying, "Son of man, raise a lament over the king of Tyre, and you must say to him, 'thus says the Lord Yahweh:
> "You were the signet of perfection,
> full of wisdom and perfect of beauty.
> **You were in Eden, the garden of God,**

and every **precious stone** was your adornment:
carnelian, topaz and moonstone,
    turquoise, onyx and jasper,
sapphire, malachite and emerald;
    and gold was the craftsmanship of your settings
    and your mountings in you;
on the day when you were created
    they were prepared.
You were an anointed guardian cherub,
    and I placed you on the **holy mountain of God;**
    you walked in the midst of stones of fire.
You were blameless in your ways
    from the day when you were created,
    until wickedness was found in you.
In the abundance of your trading,
    they filled the midst of you with violence, and you
sinned;
and I cast you as a profane thing from the **mountain
of God,**
    and I banished you, O guardian cherub,
    from the midst of the stones of fire.
Your heart was proud because of your beauty;
    you corrupted your wisdom for the sake of your
splendor.
I cast you to the ground;
    I exposed you before kings,
    to feast their eyes on you."'" (Ezekiel 28:13–17)

Now, is this talking about the king of Tyre? Or is it referring to the fall of Satan?

The king of Tyre was obviously not in Eden, the garden of God. He was not an anointed guardian cherub—Ezekiel's term for a divine throne-guardian (*cf.* Ezekiel 10). He was not placed on God's holy mountain—namely, Eden. He did not walk among stones of fire—imagery either evoking the precious stones of a palace meeting-place, or the "morning stars" themselves. None of these things were literally true of the king of Tyre.

They were literally true of Satan, the serpent, who was in Eden.

The point of Ezekiel's taunt-song is that the king of Tyre is so bad that he can be described *as if* he were Satan. There is a parallel between his hubris and Satan's; between how far his fall would be, and how far Satan's was. This parallel, then, illustrates that Satan was present in Eden—which in turn is described implicitly as the divine council meeting place.

There is another passage that uses a similar parallel to make a similar point about the king of Babylon:

> How you have fallen from heaven, O **morning star,** son of dawn!
>> You are cut down to the ground, conqueror of nations!
>
> And you said in your heart,
>> "I will ascend to heaven;
>
> I will raise up my throne above the **stars** of God;
> and I will sit on the **mountain of assembly**
>> **on the summit of Tsaphon;**
>
> I will ascend to the high places of the clouds,
>> I will make myself like the Most High." (Isaiah 14:12–14)

Isaiah is making the same point about the king of Babylon as Ezekiel makes about the king of Tyre. This time the allusion trades off more direct narratives within Canaanite religion. Mount Tsaphon is where Ba'al and his council were thought to assemble in Ugarit. Isaiah sees in this narrative a reflection of the divine coup in Eden, and so he appropriates the language of Ugaritic religion to compare the king of Babylon to Satan—who had the hubris to blaspheme God by trying to "correct" his decisions as supreme ruler.

There is some question as to correctly translating the title given to the king of Babylon/Satan here. The Hebrew is *heylel ben shachar*, which means "heylel, son of shachar." Although "morning star" is on safe footing for rendering *heylel*, this word only occurs here in the Hebrew Bible; and while *shachar* means "dawn," it was also the proper name of a Canaanite god. Some therefore see the name of a deity here: Heylel—associated with the morning star—whose father was Shachar. They further suppose that Isaiah was referring to a myth in which Heylel was thrown down from Mount Tsaphon. I demur: there is no known Canaanite deity called Heylel who was the son of Shachar; nor is there any Canaanite myth involving his being cast from Mount Tsaphon (aside from scholarly speculation). The morning star was typically represented by Shachar himself, the god of dawn—or by Attar, of whom Shachar may have been an avatar. Either way, there was no deity Heylel associated with Venus. It's true that Attar did try to fill Ba'al's shoes, but discovered he was too tiny; so he went to rule the underworld instead. Isaiah probably had this myth in mind, since the comparison is so fittingly mocking to the Babylonian king; but that cannot be the *extent* of the parallel, because Attar was not thrown down, and he didn't have the kind of pretensions that the Babylonian king had. So while there is probably a conceptual link being made to the Canaanite deity, I doubt we should translate either Heylel or Shachar as proper names. Intriguingly, the DSS differ from the MT and read היליל—*heyleyl*—rather than הילל—*heylel*—so it's possible Isaiah is actually intending a verb here instead of a noun: "wailer/howler." A rendering like, "How you are fallen from heaven, O lamenter, son of dawn," could be correct, and would still conjure up the same associations with the morning star via *shachar*.

There are further strands of evidence we can draw in at this point—additional puzzling passages that start to make a great deal of sense when we think of them in divine council terms. Firstly, in Genesis 1:26, God says, "Let us make mankind in **our** image;" and in chapter 3 he speaks of how Adam and Eve have "become like **us**, knowing good and evil."

Some think this is trinitarian language, but that makes no sense contextually; it would be meaningless—worse, confusing—to its original audience, who had no conception of trinitarian theology. Moreover, inter-trinitarian discussion like this isn't something we see elsewhere in the Bible, even in the New Testament.

Some therefore think this is a royal "we," but while Hebrew has a plural of majesty for nouns, it does not have it for verbs—and "make" in Genesis 1:26 is plural. A far simpler explanation is that God is speaking to the members of his council, which the original readers of Genesis would have assumed were present. Job 38 certainly indicates their presence at the creation of the world:

> Where were you at my laying the foundation of the earth?
>     Tell me, if you possess understanding.
> Who determined its measurement? Surely you know!
>     Or who stretched the measuring line upon it?
> On what were its bases sunk?
>     Or who laid its cornerstone,
> when the **morning stars were singing together**
>     **and all the sons of God shouted for joy?** (Job 38:4–7)

We know who the sons of God are. And we know that "morning stars" is a stock term to describe them. And that brings us to a closer look at Satan—because if you were paying attention, Isaiah 14:12 described *him* as a morning star. He was a son of God: a member of the divine council.

## THE SERPENT AS A DIVINE BEING

The obvious objection we must field now is this: Genesis describes Satan as a *serpent.* Most Christians have interpreted this as a case of animal possession—certainly not as an encounter with a divine being. How can we reconcile the serpent language of Genesis 3 with the connections I have drawn from biblical theology?

The answer is to do some more biblical theology. There are further clues we can connect across the scriptures that conceptually link the language used in Genesis 3, and the language used of the divine council elsewhere. For example, we know from Ezekiel 28 that Satan was a cherub. Chapter 1 describes these cherubs for us:

> As for the likeness of the living creatures, their appearance was like burning coals of fire, like the appearance of torches. And the living creatures were speeding to and fro like the appearance of lightning. (Ezekiel 1:13–14)

The fact that brightness is a defining feature of these creatures should come as no surprise. As Yoda would say, "Luminous beings are they." This is also hinted at in places which don't explicitly mention brightness. For example, we've seen in Isaiah 6:2 that God's throne is flanked by seraphs, sometimes spelled saraphs (many Bibles bafflingly transliterate the Hebrew plural into the Christianese: *seraphim*). This word is the same we find in Numbers 21:8–9:

> Make for yourself a fiery serpent *[saraph]* and place it on a pole. When anyone is bitten and looks at it, that person will live." So Moses made a bronze snake *[nachash]*, and he placed it on the pole; whenever a snake bit someone, and that person looked at the bronze snake, he lived. (Numbers 21:8–9)

Why is the ascription of *saraph* to the bronze snake important? Aside from the obvious serpent connection, bronze has a brightness to it. For instance, compare this with Daniel's vision:

> I lifted up my eyes and I saw, and there was a man, and he was dressed in linen, and his waist was girded with the gold of Uphaz. Now his body was like turquoise, and his face was like the appearance of lightning, and his eyes were like torches of fire, and his arms and his legs were like the **gleam of polished bronze.** (Daniel 10:5–6)

---

The text does not say that this man is an archangel, or one of the sons of God—but he is engaged in conflict with other beings we have already identified as such: the princes (or rulers) of Persia and Greece (Daniel 10:13). He appears to be a subordinate of Michael. If archangels are ontologically superior to the general armies of heaven, then we can infer that a being who can engage in extended conflict with them is surely on a similar level. If archangels are ontologically identical to the rest of the angelic army, and simply hold a greater rank—as is the case with human armies—then the point is moot. Either way, the man who visits Daniel is the same kind of being as an archangel.

---

Notice how this archangel is described with the likeness of shining metal. He, like Moses' saraph, is brazen. Already there is an obvious conceptual connection—but it goes further than this, because the "gleam of polished bronze" here in Daniel is, in Hebrew, *nechoshet*. This word is derived from *nachash*—the Hebrew term interchanged with *saraph* in Numbers 21:8–9, and the word translated "serpent" in Genesis 3:1ff. Like some English words (*e.g., express* and *home), nachash* can be a noun, it can be a verb, or it can be an adjective.

- As a noun, *nachash* means serpent.
- As a verb, *nachash* means to divine; "the *nachash*" means the diviner.
- As an adjective, *nachash* means shining (as bronze); "the *nachash*" means the shining one.[1]

We know from Ezekiel and from Isaiah that seraphs have a shining appearance. We know from Exodus that a seraph is serpentine, and that its shining appearance is associated with bronze. We know from Daniel that archangels have a shining, bronze-like appearance that is described with the same root word as *nachash*. And we know that the serpent of Genesis 3 was a *nachash*. Thus, there is a kind of conceptual nexus involving *saraph* and *nachash*, evoking a serpentine form and a luminous, brazen appearance. Although these terms *can*

---

1. If you would like to check my working on all this, see Michael S. Heiser, "The Nachash (נָחָשׁ) and His Seed: Some Explanatory Notes on Why the 'Serpent' in Genesis 3 Wasn't a Serpent": http://www.pidradio.com/wp-content/uploads/2007/02/nachashnotes.pdf.

refer to mundane snakes, they also seem to refer to luminous, serpentine beings which surround or guard the throne of God. Beings very much like the winged, serpentine gods of Egypt, depicted flanking the thrones of Pharaohs.

Simply put, the clues in Scripture do not lead us to a possessed snake in Genesis 3. The memes in the minds of the original readers point us in quite another direction:

> The serpent was not a snake, but rather a luminous serpentine being—one of the council of God.

But how can we square this with Genesis 3:1, 14? Do they not clearly identify the serpent as a beast of the field? Let's consider this objection in two parts:

### 1. *The serpent is compared to the beasts*

Many translations render the serpent as more cunning and more cursed than any *other* beast (*e.g.*, ESV, LEB, NLT). But the Hebrew does not necessitate such a translation: it can simply mean that he was shrewder than *any* beast (so NET, NIV, NASB). This part of the objection actually trips over what looks like a *deliberate* conflation on Moses' part: if his audience would have immediately understood that the *nachash* was *not* a beast, then Genesis 3:1 is really a bit of laconic humor, playing off the triple entendre. Thus, I don't think the comparison to the beasts of the field is for the purpose of *identifying* the serpent at all, but rather to create a rhetorical contrast between him, the couple, and the animals. This occurs through two ironic reversals:

1.  In Hebrew word translated "cunning"—perhaps better "shrewd" or "wiley"—is *arum*. The term behind "naked" is *arummim*. And "cursed" is *arur*. The words are all related, creating a wordplay: the serpent starts out *arum*, in a position of power over the couple who are *arummim*; but he ends up *arur*, in a position of lowest disgrace. He aims to get dominion over them, but ends up being made lower even than the animals *they* have dominion over.

2.  This is further emphasized by the ambiguity of *nachash*, which frames the serpent superficially in the role of a beast. This magnifies the reversal of authority at the heart of the fall: the creation usurps the couple who were given rule over it, the woman usurps the man who was given rule over her, and the man usurps God who rules over all.

### 2. *The serpent goes on his belly*

Genesis 3:14b is also often taken to show that this is how snakes became belly-crawling dirt-eaters. (For the record, I do not understand the insistence of translators in rendering *apar* as dust rather than dirt, as if you could mold dust into the shape of a man; the name *adam*, man, plays on *adamah*, ground, along with *edom*, red—so dirt or soil is a much better and more obvious translation of *apar* than dust in this instance.) But nothing in the text makes sense of treating it as an etiological fable—that is simply not the point of it, even if snakes *did* eat dirt. And since they don't, the fable would strictly speaking be false. So this phrase is surely metaphorical, referring to complete disgrace and subjugation—as it does in places like Micah 7:17; Psalm 72:9; Isaiah 49:23, and just general usage, even in English!

But if eating dirt is metaphorical, then so presumably is going on his belly: it is a parallelism that likewise refers to being made low. This makes clear sense, given that prostrating oneself was exactly how one indicated complete deference and submission in the ancient Near East (*cf.* Psalm 44:25; 119:25; Lamentations 3:16). Indeed, if Genesis 3 was written on the tail of leaving Egypt, its original audience would never have thought to read "go on your belly" as a loss of limbs—they would have been familiar with such language since it was common in Egypt, where spells against serpents would command them to do this exact thing. A serpent rampant is raised up and threatening to bite; a serpent recumbent is unable to do so. Thus, the curse on the serpent would be read as a restraint on Satan's combative power for the sake of his weaker foe, humanity.[2] This cashes out in three ways that unfold through redemptive history:

1. **A change of domain.** We've seen how Isaiah 14:12–15 speaks of Satan being fallen from heaven and cut down to the earth. Similarly, Job 1:7; 1 Peter 5:8 show us the earth as his domain; he spends his time here in the dirt.

2. **A commensurate change in honor.** Although he is still by nature a god, he is both disgraced and sentenced to die. So despite being respected for *what* he is (*cf.* Jude 1:8–10), he is despised and dishonored for *who* he is (*cf.* John 8:44).

3. **A complete eschatological subjugation.** I'll cover this in depth in the coming chapters; suffice to say for now that since the cross, Satan is subjugated under a *man*—

2. John H. Walton, *Genesis* (Zondervan, 2001), 224-25, cited by Steve Hays, "He shall bruise your head and you shall bruise his heel" on Triablogue (August 2017): https://triablogue.blogspot.com/2017/08/he-shall-bruise-your-head-and-you-shall.html.

Jesus—who will one day judge him and sentence him to the second death. Thus the ironic reversal for him becomes complete (*cf.* Psalm 8:5).

These factors all line up to make an animal interpretation of the serpent very awkward—regardless of whether we see the snake as possessed by Satan, or simply an agent on his behalf. The latter understanding is certainly *more* awkward, though it is certainly venerable, being reflected in Jubilees 3:28 and Josephus.[3] For the sake of completeness, and because much rides on correctly identifying the serpent before we move on, let me briefly outline the major reasons it makes no sense.

1.  **The curse does not include a removal of speech.** When God curses the serpent and the couple, he is quite specific about what is going to happen. These specifics do not include removing the ability to talk—neither for the serpent, nor for animals in general.

2.  **There's no clear reason for a talking animal to tempt the couple.** Genesis says the serpent was shrewd, but what is shrewd about him trying to get the couple executed if he was just an animal? What would he have to gain by that? Conversely, there is every reason for a member of God's heavenly council to tempt them: he is motivated by envy. Adam was given dominion over the world despite being made lower than the angels—so it's easy to see how a high-ranking angel like the serpent would bristle at this, and plot to have Adam executed so dominion could "rightfully" pass to him.

3.  **Snakes are not the particular enemies of people.** There are many species of animals which are far more in-

---

3. Josephus, *Antiquities of the Jews,* 1:1.4: https://www.biblestudytools.com/history/flavius-josephus/antiquities-jews/book-1/chapter-1.html.

clined to attack humans; snakes typically avoid us. For our own part, arachnophobia is far more prevalent than ophidiophobia. More crucially, a literal interpretation of the enmity between the seed of the serpent and the seed of the woman eliminates the Protevangelium—the first announcement of the gospel! It turns Genesis 3:15 into a pointless remark about animals that has no connection to the outcome of the struggle between the sons of the devil and the Son of God.

Reading the Bible like a newspaper is destructive to the meaning of the text—and also to the effort of making and keeping disciples. By turning Genesis 3 into something like a faerie story, we dull ourselves to the subtle rhetorical ironies and contrasts in the text, and replace a grown-up theology with something more like skim milk. As Ron Swanson would say, in an admittedly different context, there's only one thing I hate more than lying, and that's skim milk—which is water lying about being milk.

## SATAN AND ADAM AS RIVALS FOR RULERSHIP

As long as the divine council only comprised God and his spiritual household, they would logically commune in their natural state: a disembodied form perhaps akin to a shared dream. But if God wished to add Adam to his council, and do so in a way that intersected with Adam's normal mode of existence, then the whole council would need to be physically perceptible in a physical location, where Adam could interact with them. Hence the garden of Eden.

This being so, the subplot of Genesis 1–3 is not too hard to discern. Why does Satan tempt Adam and Eve? Presumably because he wants them dead; he knows God has given the death penalty for disobedience (Genesis 2:17). Why does he want them dead? Well, the chief point of the creation account is that Adam and Eve get dominion over the world. Yet that's odd given the existence of superior beings like Satan. We know that God made us a little *lower* than the *elohim*, the gods (Psalm 8:5; *cf.* Hebrews 2:7)—so giving us dominion seems backwards. Satan naturally expected to get rulership of the world himself. He was the superior being. You put the greatest in charge. The angel of angels. How dare God give the world to a pathetic creature like Adam?

Admittedly it is difficult to finesse Satan's motivations, since we don't know what it's like to be a spiritual being. How can we put ourselves in the shoes of someone who doesn't have any? That said, given the information at hand, I don't think Satan cared about Adam's dominion per se—about ordering the plant and animal life and bending it to his will. Rather, I suspect he was interested in ordering *man* and bending him to his will. Thus, if we want to be very specific, Satan's beef was likely not so much with Adam getting dominion over the earth, but with him *not* getting dominion over Adam. It would be fine for Adam to be "head beast" over all the other beasts—but a viceroy of God? Not answerable to Satan? That would rankle—which suggests that Satan's rebellion was even more a case of cutting off his nose to spite his face than it first appears. Not only was he rebelling, ultimately, against God, which he had to know was a bad idea, but he didn't even want what Adam had! He just wanted *Adam* under his thumb; not the world. But if he couldn't have that, he'd rather see Adam dead and get the world anyway.

That's my speculation. We aren't told what Satan's plans were. And it doesn't really matter to us at this point; the key issue is that we don't need to read very far between the lines of Genesis to see a plot to eliminate Adam. We can suppose at the very least that Satan had a difference of opinion with God as to the propriety of a lesser being holding authority, rather than a greater one—so he tried to stage a coup. With Adam out of the way, God would restore dominion to its "proper" order by putting Satan in charge.

Now, given that he *has* dominion over man, you might think his plan succeeded—but it didn't. Not at first. To understand this, we need to now examine the fallout of the curse.

# CHAPTER 4
# A TALE OF TWO SEEDS

*The fallout of the curse was a bitter war between the seed of the serpent, and the seed of the woman, within the one kingdom God had established. This culminated at Babel, where Yahweh disinherited mankind and divided them among the sons of God—taking Israel as his kingdom and giving the rest to Satan.*

God has created something new: a world made of matter. He has created new family members out of this matter, to represent him in this new world. And he has put them in a place where they can meet his existing family members, who are not made of matter: the sons of God. Together, they will constitute a ruling family-council. When Adam is ready, he will be given the knowledge required to rule well—the knowledge of good and evil (I Kings 3:7–10)—and take charge of the world as king in God's stead.

The serpent, hoping to have rulership of the world passed to him, tempts Adam to get himself executed by defying God. As a trusted member of God's court—indeed, a patriarch in his spiritual household—he is able to trick Eve into disobedience, which in turn sways Adam. But this plan to wrest dominion of the world backfires badly. In Genesis 3:14–15, not only is Adam not executed as the serpent expected, and he himself is not put in charge, but God rather ironically reverses Satan's pretensions: promising to make him of less worth than not just Adam, but even the animals. Worse—he promises Eve a descendant to mortally wound him!

## THE ONGOING CORRUPTION

We discover that God uses *death* as a term to describe not summary execution, but separation—Adam dies by being separated from God (*cf.* John 1:4; Revelation 2:11; 21:8), and thus his body will eventually expire, as a flower will eventually wither when cut from the root. But although Adam is kicked out of Eden, and doesn't have access to God's council any longer, he retains dominion over the world. That is part of the creation—the *dominion*—mandate. It is the command, the purpose, given to man at creation. It is not rescinded in the curse; it is only made more difficult.

He goes out, and he is fruitful and multiplies, and he rules over the beasts of the field and the birds of the air and the fish of the sea.

But the serpent and his cronies are not so easily deterred. Indeed, they are pot-committed. And so in Genesis 6 we see something really weird happen—something that surely is directly related to the curse on the serpent, which says:

> I will put enmity between you and the woman,
> and between your seed and her seed;
> he shall strike your head,
> and you shall strike his heel. (Genesis 3:15)

We tend to interpret "seed" here as referring to *spiritual* offspring. This is certainly a legitimate gloss—Jesus himself interprets it this way when he calls the Pharisees sons of the devil in John 8:44 (*cf.* Matthew 23:33 etc). Either God is your Father, or the devil is:

> Little children, let no one deceive you. Whoever practices righteousness is righteous, as he is righteous. Whoever makes a practice of sinning is of the devil, for the devil has been sinning from the beginning. The reason the Son of God appeared was to destroy the works of the devil. No one born of God makes a practice of sinning, for God's **seed** abides in him; and he cannot keep on sinning, because he has been born of God. By this it is evident who are the children of God, and who are the children of the devil: whoever does not practice righteousness is not of God, nor is the one who does not love his brother. (1 John 3:7–10)

If you are born of the flesh, you are born of Adam, and God puts you under the adoption of the devil, the serpent. If you are reborn of spirit (John 3:5), you are born of Jesus, into God's family, and the Father adopts you as his own children.

But how did this happen? How—more importantly why—are those in Adam under the adoption of the *serpent?* It cannot merely be because they do the works of the serpent, and sonship involves taking up the work of your father. Adoption doesn't happen on the basis of the works of the child; rather, the works of the child are evidence of who has already taken him as a son. Adoption is legal—or, biblically speaking, covenantal. So how did reprobate man come under the adoption of Satan?

It starts in Genesis 6, with a seed that is not *merely* spiritual:

> And it happened that, when man began to multiply on the face of the land, daughters were born to them. Then the sons of God saw the daughters of man, that they were beautiful. And they took for themselves

> wives from all that they chose. And Yahweh said, "My Spirit shall not abide with man forever in that he is also flesh. And his days shall be one hundred and twenty years." The Nephilim were upon the earth in those days, and also afterward, when the sons of God went into the daughters of man, and they bore children to them. These were the mighty warriors that were from ancient times, men of renown.
>
> And Yahweh saw that the evil of man was great upon the earth, and every inclination of the thoughts of his heart was nothing but evil continually. And Yahweh regretted that he had made man on the earth, and he was grieved in his heart. And Yahweh said, "I will destroy man whom I created from upon the face of the earth, from man, to beasts, to creeping things, and to the birds of heaven, for I regret that I have made them." But Noah found favor in his eyes. (Genesis 6:1–8)

Now *what* is going on here? We aren't given all the details, but we do see that some of the sons of God take human wives. They sire a physical seed to compete with the line of Eve—giant half-breeds who are later named as Israel's special enemies (Numbers 13:33).[1] Evil and violence subsequently get so bad that God determines to destroy the entire world, leaving only one loyal survivor and his family.

In 1 Enoch, which I believe preserves a legitimately ancient though embellished tradition, the sons of God—there called the watchers, as in Daniel—are responsible for greatly increasing the depravity of man by teaching them things like sorcery and astrology. This is a prime motivation for the Flood, which otherwise is somewhat puzzling in terms of its timing, given that

---

1. For a more detailed defense of the Jewish view of Genesis 6, see my exchange with Steve Hays of Triablogue: D. Bnonn Tennant, "What is Genesis 6:1–4 talking about?" (March 2015): https://bnonn.com/what-is-genesis-61-4-talking-about/.

mankind was corrupt from Eden. It also explains several threads in the New Testament that play off Enochian material, where Jesus is implicitly depicted as reversing the sins of the watchers.[2]

It's easy to rabbit-trail on titillating narratives like this—but the only thing we need to know for understanding the kingdom of God is that Genesis 6 is a milestone in the long and sordid relationship between mankind and the sons of God. This relationship does not end at the Flood, but in fact continues directly after it, with another event that Christians find rather puzzling: Babel. As the population of the earth increases, the people gather together and say to each other, "Come, let us build ourselves a city and a tower whose top reaches to the heavens. And let us make a name for ourselves, lest we be scattered over the face of the whole earth" (Genesis 11:4).

We tend to read this as if the people at Babel were trying to literally climb into heaven by building a super-tall tower. But this is not what was going on. As we've seen already, the ancient worldview connected high places with divine presence. Mountains were where heaven and earth connected. Thus, artificial mountains were a standard feature of religious practice. This was the purpose of Mesopotamian ziggurats: to establish a place where the gods could be sought; where they would presence themselves. And we have good reasons to think that the tower of Babel was in fact a ziggurat—possibly the model for the famous ziggurat in Babylon known as Etemenanki.[3]

---

2. Since this is somewhat tangential I won't discuss it further here, but for a stimulating exercise in biblical theology and contextual exegesis, see Michael S. Heiser, *Reversing Hermon: Enoch, the Watchers, and the Forgotten Mission of Jesus Christ* (Defender Publishing, 2017).

3. John H. Walton, "Is there Archaeological Evidence for the Tower of Babel?" on Associates for Biblical Research (May 2008): http://www.biblearchaeology.org/post/2008/05/Is-there-Archaeological-Evidence-for-the-Tower-of-Babel.aspx.

The point that Genesis is making is that the people are not honoring God. They are not enacting the creation mandate under his governance. They are refusing to carry God's name into the world—indeed, they are refusing to even spread out and multiply and fill the earth. They are choosing, instead, to stay in one place in order to build up their *own* name and retake *heaven* by reestablishing contact with the sons of God. Babel is thus effectively an attempted coup, where mankind seeks to join forces with their "allies" against Yahweh in the divine council, to set up a rival power base for rulership of the cosmos.

Interestingly, Babylonian mythology puts a positive spin on this event, representing the sons of God, the Apkallu, as the ones who founded Babylon and imparted knowledge of culture and technology.[4] Second Temple Jewish writings put rather a different gloss on it: the Apkallu were the ones who taught mankind things like idolatry and witchcraft. It is because of them that, at Babel, humanity actively rejects God's rule, and seeks instead other divine beings.

Put simply, mankind refuses to rule *on behalf* of God—to act as his viceroys, his representatives on earth. They want to image other gods, and serve them instead.

Although Adam *ruined* his representation of God by inverting the creation authority structure, he nonetheless *retained* that representation. He kept the right to rule in God's stead, even though he and his kingdom were des-

<hr>

4. Amar Annus, "On the Origin of Watchers: A Comparative Study of the Antediluvian Wisdom in Mesopotamian and Jewish Traditions," *Journal for the Study of the Pseudepigrapha* (volume 19, issue 4) (2010), 277–20): https://www.scribd.com/doc/165671817/277-full-pdf.

ecrated by the fall; unable to properly image God or remain in his presence. Babel presupposes that this original kingdom structure is still in place: it presents us with a united community migrating east until they settle in Shinar (Genesis 11:1–2), who are "one people" (v. 6). God is still, in principle, the direct ruler over this united people, and they in turn have a single territory—the earth. But at Babel, they actively *refuse* God's rule. They will not represent him; they want instead to represent other gods. They declare war on God's throne.

Now, what is God to do here? He has promised that he will not wipe the slate clean and start again (Genesis 9:11). The only real option left is to finally give mankind over to what they want (*cf.* Romans 1:21–25).

## THE DISINHERITANCE OF MANKIND

Up until this point, the world has been one kingdom: the kingdom of God. Yahweh was its king; mankind his viceroy and his people; the earth their territory. But at Babel, God must do something about their rebellion, and so he separates this kingdom into two: his kingdom, and the kingdom of Satan. Both kingdoms exist alongside each other; Adam's kingdom is subdivided, as it were, into Israel and the world:

> When the Most High gave to the nations their inheritance,
> > when he divided mankind,
> he fixed the borders of the peoples
> > according to the number of the sons of God.
> But Yahweh's portion is his people,
> > Jacob his allotted heritage. (Deuteronomy 32:8–9)

The passage is an antithetic parallelism, contrasting the statements of verses 8 and 9, as indicated by the "but." The structure demands that what is true in the relationship of verse 9 is also at least broadly true of the relationship in verse 8—only in reversed order, due to the chiasmus. If we think of Hebrew as rhyming ideas rather than sounds, it is an ABBA rhyme-scheme. (The reading of v. 8a is also ambiguous; syntactically, it could be "gave the nations *as* an inheritance," which certainly makes more sense of the parallelism; I think both are true and the ambiguity is intentional.) This establishes the following contrast:

A. Yahweh gave an inheritance to/of the nations
B. He apportioned the nations according to the number of the sons of God
B. But his portion is his people
A. He took an inheritance of Israel

The parallelism requires that what is true between Israel and Yahweh also be true between the peoples and the sons of God; thus, Moses here glosses Babel as a *disinheritance* of the nations: God allots territories to the divided peoples in accordance with his allotment of the peoples themselves to the sons of God. The picture is that of Luke 15:12, in which the contemptuous son demands his inheritance early—saying to his father, in effect, "I wish you were dead." Indeed, the parable of the prodigal, though individualized, is set within a discourse on the *kingdom,* and is surely Jesus' gloss on Babel—and on how his gospel is going to reverse it. Mankind should have inherited the whole world as a unified kingdom under God: the earth was Adam's inheritance. But they insisted on another path, and squandered that inheritance.

So God divides the world among them (*cf.* for instance Numbers 2:1–23)...and then he washes his hands of them. They have disowned him; he therefore disowns them, and thus their right to represent him. He will no longer rule *over* them (directly), but they will no longer rule *for* him. Rather, he gives them what they demanded: an alliance with, and subjection to, other gods. He apportions Adam's kingdom to the archangels; he removes mankind's presumptive adoption as his children, and makes them adoptive children of another disowned son: the serpent.

Thus, the archangels become their new gods, and Satan becomes the ruler and god of this world over them. This is the clear picture that emerges once we combine the clues in the Old Testament with the New Testament's witness to Satan being in charge; there isn't any doubt that he is the serpent of Genesis, since Revelation 20:2 explicitly says so.

---

Many translations of Deuteronomy 32:8–9 follow the Masoretic Text (c. 1,000 AD), which reads "sons of Israel" rather than "sons of God." That this is a later interpretive alteration is obvious when we compare the LXX and DSS on this point. The LXX itself gives a dynamic translation that goes the other way (ἀγγέλων θεοῦ, angels of God), and some versions say υἱῶν θεοῦ, sons of God; a straight, formal translation of בני אלהים or בני אל, *beney elohim* or *beney el*, which are both attested at Qumran. Aside from the exegetical issues I adduce below, the MT's gloss is clearly wrong since Israel did not exist at the time described: its origin is at some point *after* Babel, and it is not included on the table of nations in Genesis 10.

---

Deuteronomy 32:8–9 has a conceptual parallel in Deuteronomy 4:19–20. Whereas the former describes the nations being given over to *elohim* who were not Yahweh, the latter describes the other side of the punitive coin:

> And beware lest you lift up your eyes to heaven, and when you see the sun and the moon and the stars, all the host of heaven [צבא השמים—*tsaba ha'shamayim*, the standard nomenclature for the armies of heaven], you be drawn away and bow down to them and serve them, which Yahweh your God has allotted [חלק] to all the peoples under the whole heaven. But Yahweh took [לקח] you and brought you out of the iron furnace, out

> of Egypt, to be a people of his own inheritance, as you are this day. (Deuteronomy 4:19–20; *cf.* Deuteronomy 29:26)

Notice again the parallelism, emphasized by the wordplay between *chalaq* and *laqach*: God has taken Israel as his own inheritance, but allotted the nations to the heavenly host (by parallel, also as an inheritance).

God does not disown *all* mankind. He keeps Israel—starting with just Abraham—as his portion, as his kingdom, to rule over and to rule for him. The rest gets broken up by tongue, according to the number of the sons of God. Presumably this is idiomatic, not meant to be taken as there being only 70 archangels as per the family history of the nations in Genesis 10; we see elsewhere that nations have multiple gods, which fits the dynastic, household structure of the system (*e.g.,* Exodus 12:12); moreover, the Bible's focus is limited to the nations Israel would be dealing with, and doesn't take account of more remote areas around the rest of the globe.

This event, this divvying of Adam's kingdom, is why Genesis 11 leads straight into the call of Abram. It is the story of God creating his *own* kingdom in competition with Satan's. By the same token, Deuteronomy 32:8–9 is an *explanation* of Israel's existence—and what it is up against.

This also explains other parts of the Bible which are typically glossed over—or argued over. Once we have this overarching structure in place, many otherwise confounding details of Scripture become clear, while other seemingly mundane details take on new meaning. A couple of examples will suffice; once you have internalized this material and become fluent in spotting patterns and symbols in Scripture, you will find them everywhere:

1. In Exodus 12:12, Yahweh cryptically remarks that he is going to execute judgments on the gods of Egypt as he passes through the land in the final plague. One does not punish non-existent beings. These were, in fact, the sons of God who had given Pharaoh's magicians the power to turn staffs into snakes (Exodus 7:10–12) and water into blood (v. 22). The notion that ancient people were slobbering cavemen who got so frightened by thunder that they had to invent gods to appease is not a product of careful historical study, but blind chronological snobbery. They were not worshiping non-existent gods with non-existent power—they were worshiping real gods with real power.

2. The battle between David and Goliath takes on far greater significance, both in terms of simple history, and in terms of prophetic imaging. Goliath, the giant enemy of God's people, descended from the line of the serpent, was mortally wounded by David, the man after God's own heart, anointed to be king, from whose line came Jesus.

This, conveniently enough, also returns us to the point at hand—what God is doing about Satan's rulership of the world. Psalm 82:8 says:

> Rise up, O God—judge the earth,
> for you shall inherit all the nations.

Even in the conquest of Canaan, Israel failed to do a perfect job. And things pretty much got worse from there on out. As a kingdom representing God's rule on earth, it ranged between less than perfect on its best days, and downright detestable for most of its sad history. Ultimately, Israel refused God's rule in exactly the way the residents of Babel did: through repeated and insistent idolatry. Therefore, God scattered them into the nations he had already disowned.

By the time of the New Testament, God's kingdom had largely been dispersed among the nations; the small remnant that remained was under the rulership of the foreign nation of Rome—which meant it was under the direct power of *Satan* (*cf.* Revelation 2:13; 3:9). As we'll see, this is why demon-possession is such a major feature of the synoptic gospels, whereas it never shows up in the Old Testament: what we have in the 400 years between Malachi and Matthew is the occupation of Israel by hostile spiritual forces, and the complete collapse of God's kingdom.

Yet this was, in fact, all part of the plan. God intended to retake *all* the nations. In weakness, his strength would be perfected; the dismantling of his kingdom by Satan and the sons of God was, ironically, the very mechanism of their undoing. As he had disowned the nations, so he intended to own them again. Not just Israel: as Psalm 82 says, he plans to reclaim *every* nation from the rulership of the corrupt gods, and judge those gods for their rule.

Knowing this, we are now ready to move into the New Testament—and ultimately, to the modern day. This is where everything we've talked about starts to come together. Cosmology. The divine council. Geography and sacred space. Physical imaging of spiritual archetypes.

# CHAPTER 5

# WHEN GOD BEGAN RETAKING ADAM'S KINGDOM FROM SATAN

*Before we can understand how God is retaking Adam's kingdom, we must first establish when he began to do it. Daniel 7 was fulfilled after Pentecost when Jesus went into heaven on a cloud and received kingship to place his enemies under his feet.*

In Daniel 2, Nebuchadnezzar dreams of a great statue, representing four kingdoms. The first kingdom is definitely Babylon, and the second definitely includes Persia; but scholars quibble over the divisions from there on out.

I believe we can say with confidence that, despite what many scholars prefer, the second kingdom is Media-Persia, the third Greece, and the fourth Rome. The reason for having such confidence about the identity of the fourth kingdom is this: Reading verse 44, we learn that in the day of its kings, "the God of heaven will set up a kingdom that will never be destroyed, and the kingdom will not be left for another nation, and it will bring an end to all these kingdoms, but it will stand forever."

As I will now set out to show, this describes the work of Jesus in history, at the height of the Roman empire.

I'm going to focus on the evidence in the New Testament rather than the evidence of Roman history, but the latter is worth studying also to reinforce the case.

These same four kingdoms appear—or perhaps more correctly, the powers behind them appear—in the beginning of Daniel 7. This time they are represented as four beasts. Daniel is considering the horns of the fourth beast, which represent kings (Daniel 7:24), when the scene changes to the divine courtroom:

> I continued watching until thrones were placed and an Ancient of Days sat; his clothing was like white snow and the hair of his head was like pure wool and his throne was a flame of fire and its wheels were burning fire. A stream of fire issued forth and flowed from his presence; thousands upon thousands served him and ten thousand upon ten thousand stood before him. The judge sat, and the books were opened.
>
> I continued watching then because of the noise of the boastful words of the horn who was speaking; I continued watching until the beast was slain and its body was destroyed, and it was given over to burning with fire. And as for the remainder of the beasts, their dominion was taken away, but a prolongation of their life was given to them for a season and a time.
>
> I continued watching in the visions of the night, and look, with the clouds of heaven one like a son of man was coming, and he came to the Ancient of Days, and was presented before him. And to him was given dominion and glory and kingship that all the peoples, the nations, and languages would serve him; his dominion is a dominion without end that will not cease, and his kingdom is one that will not be destroyed. (Daniel 7:9–14)

Here we see the heavenly event which ushers in the kingdom promised in Daniel 2:44 during the time of the fourth kingdom. But before we link this to the New Testament, there is one other very remarkable detail that comes shortly afterward—a critical clue to how the kingdom of God unfolds in the church age:

> These great beasts which are four in number are four kings who will arise from the earth. But the holy ones of the Most High will receive the kingdom, and they will take possession of the kingdom forever—forever and ever. (Daniel 7:18)

We have seen that "holy ones" is a common term used to describe divine beings, the sons of God—especially when linked to terms like "the Most High." But clearly *these* holy ones are *not* divine beings: the whole point of Daniel 7:18; 22; 27 is that the holy ones are given rulership or possession of the kingdom of God, which they do not yet have; and this stands in obvious contrast to the rulership or possession of the nations, which the sons of God currently *do* have. What we see in Daniel 7 is a therefore changeover from the old dominion we've seen in the previous chapters, to a new one. The rulership of the nations is stripped from the gods, taken over by the Son of Man, and subsumed into an eternal kingdom that will never end.

This leaves only one likely group these holy ones could be: **God's human people.**

That these holy ones are human is reflected in translations like the ESV, which renders it *saints*. A much better way of approaching this, however, is to simply do away with the word saints altogether; the New Testament word ἅγιοι literally *means* "holy ones," so translating it into Christianese instead of plain English obscures the link and trajectory between the Old and New Testaments here. The same goes for ἐκκλησία, which should be translated assembly or congregation rather than church. These are terms laden with meaning in the Old Testament, so using different English words for them when we come to the New Testament makes it much harder to see how the plan of redemption plays out: the use of the *same terms* for the divine council and God's human people is of enormous theological significance—and is heavily obscured in most translations.

Bear in mind this connection of holy ones to God's people as we move forward—because as we'll see, it is the very *telos* of the gospel: the transfer of dominion from the holy assembly in the heavens to the holy assembly on earth. For now, the big question is:

When does the Son of Man come on the clouds of heaven to take possession of the eternal kingdom, as depicted in Daniel 7?

When does Jesus receive dominion and glory and kingship, that all the peoples and nations and languages should serve him? When does he become the ruler of this eternal kingdom that will never be destroyed and never come to an end?

Well, this question has become clouded—pun very much intended—by the rise of eschatological systems which interpret all the New Testament language about the Son of Man coming on the clouds as references to the *parousia*—that future time when Jesus will return to earth to judge the living and the dead. But this won't do, because Daniel explicitly places the advent of the eternal kingdom at the time of the fourth kingdom. Whether this fourth kingdom is Greece *or* Rome, it is either way an event far back in history. There is simply no millennia-long gap in Daniel's timeline.

Jesus himself explicitly clarifies the timeline in Mark 14:62, when he tells the high priest: "*you* will see the Son of Man seated at the right hand of power and coming with the clouds of heaven" (*cf.* Psalm 110:1 in addition to Daniel 7:13–14). Similarly, in Matthew 16:28 he tells his disciples, "Truly, I say to you, there are some standing here who will not taste death until they see the Son of Man coming in his kingdom." And in the Olivet Discourse, he foretells the destruction of Jerusalem and the tribulation that will follow, before concluding:

> **Immediately after the tribulation of those days** the sun will be darkened, and the moon will not give its light, and the stars will fall from heaven, and the powers of the heavens will be shaken. Then will appear in heaven the sign of the Son of Man, and then all the tribes of the earth will mourn, and they will see the Son of Man coming on the clouds of heaven with power and great glory. And he will send out his angels with a loud trumpet call, and they will gather his elect from the four winds, from one end of heaven to the other.
>
> From the fig tree learn its lesson: as soon as its branch becomes tender and puts out its leaves, you know that summer is near. So also, when you see all these things, you know that he is near, at the very gates. Truly, I say to you, **this generation will not pass away until all these things take place.** (Matthew 24:29–34; par. Mark 13:24–30; Luke 21:25–32)

Matthew, Mark and Luke all explicitly say that the generation of Jesus' day would not pass away until all these things took place. And indeed, how could they—for if this were all still to happen, even today, Jesus would still be waiting to usher in the kingdom of God. But Ephesians 1:20–22 says that God has *already* "seated him at his right hand in the heavenly places, far above all rule and authority and power and dominion, and above every name that is named, not only in this age but also in the one to come. And he put all things under his feet." 1 Corinthians 15:27 and 1 Peter 3:22 also explicitly identify this as a done deal; a finished event.

But what of the cosmic signs—the sun and the moon and the stars being darkened? Surely that is future language depicting the end of the world? Well, look at how Peter recapitulates this language in Acts 2:19–21:

> And I will show wonders in the heavens above and signs on the earth below: blood, and fire, and vapor of smoke; the sun shall be turned to darkness and the moon to blood, before the day of the Lord comes, the great and magnificent day. And it shall come to pass that everyone who calls upon the name of the Lord shall be saved. (Acts 2:19–21)

Is this speaking of Jesus returning to earth amid a literally darkened sun, blood moons, volcanoes and red tides? To answer straightforwardly, notice that Peter links these things all together: the signs, the day of the Lord, and the universal gospel call. Everyone calling on the name of the Lord is *conterminous* with these other events. Now, everyone calling on the name of the Lord is what was happening at Pentecost; it is illustrated in people from every *nation* calling on the name of the Lord. That is ongoing from then until now. But in that case, the day of the Lord has come—and the apocalyptic signs either didn't actually happen as predicted...or the Bible is not supposed to be read like a modern newspaper.

Now consider Isaiah 13—an oracle against Babylon. In the midst of the language about how Yahweh is going to summon armies against Babylon and crush it decisively, we read this:

> Behold, the day of Yahweh is coming,
>     cruel, with wrath and fierce anger,
> to make the land a desolation
>     and to destroy its sinners from it.
> For the stars of the heavens and their constellations
>     will not shine their light;

the sun will be dark at its rising,
    and the moon will not shed its light.
And I will punish the world for its evil,
    and the wicked for their iniquity;
And I will put an end to the pride of the arrogant,
    and I will bring the haughtiness of tyrants low.
I will make people more rare than fine gold,
    and man than the gold of Ophir.
Therefore I will make the heavens tremble,
    and the earth will quake from its place,
because of the wrath of Yahweh of armies
    and in the day his anger burns. (Isaiah 13:9–11)

Clearly there are eschatological overtones here, but the immediate prophecy is about Babylon—the historical empire. The oracle was fulfilled when that historical empire fell to Persia in 539 BC. Did the sun and the moon and the stars go dark back then—or did Isaiah mean for us to understand his poetic language...poetically? By the same token, take Ezekiel's lamentation over the king of Egypt, which is even more extreme: in Ezekiel 32:5–8, not only are the same signs in the heavens prophesied, but also Pharaoh's flesh being strewn on the mountains and his blood through the ravines.

Should we imagine these things literally happened? Of course not; the language is hyperbolic metaphor. In the case of the luminaries, these represent political powers; the descriptions of cosmic upheaval are *images* of political upheaval in both the spiritual and the human realms, owing to the connection between the luminaries and gods (*e.g.*, Deuteronomy 4:19; Psalm 148:3; but *cf.* also Genesis 37:9), and between spiritual conflicts and terrestrial warfare (*e.g.*, 2 Kings 6:17). Just as in Psalm 82, where bad rule shakes the foundations of the earth—not at all meaning the literal planet, but rather the world of men—so in these other passages, the heavenly bodies are undone—not at all meaning the literal stellar objects, but rather the spiritual powers.

Put succinctly, the images of cosmic upheaval are exactly the metaphors the Bible *would* use to describe a shakeup in the heavenly realms. It is precisely the kind of language we should *expect* of one ruler triumphing or conquering—especially when that ruler is God.

Although the prophetic language of Scripture is primarily symbolic here, that doesn't exclude more literal fulfillments. Jewish historian Josephus, writing in AD 75, records some truly remarkable signs prior to the destruction of Jerusalem.[1] Apart from a sword-shaped star hanging over Jerusalem, earthquakes, and a cow giving birth to a lamb at the altar, the signs he records are also summarized by Roman historian Tacitus (AD 115) as follows:

> There had been seen hosts joining battle in the skies, the fiery gleam of arms, the temple illuminated by a sudden radiance from the clouds. The doors of the inner shrine were suddenly thrown open, and a voice of more than mortal tone was heard to cry that the gods were departing. At the same instant there was a mighty stir as of departure. Some few put a fearful meaning on these events, but in most there was a firm persuasion, that in the ancient records of their priests was contained a prediction of how at this very time the East was to grow powerful, and rulers, coming from Judaea, were to acquire universal empire.[2]

The irony, of course, is that the priests were not wrong about the import of these signs. This is how Jesus can have confidence that Caiaphas and the chief priests will

1. Josephus, *The Wars of the Jews, or The History of the Destruction of Jerusalem,* 6:5.3–4: https://www.gutenberg.org/files/2850/2850-h/2850-h.htm#link62HCH0005.

2. Tacitus, *Histories,* 5:13: http://www.sacred-texts.com/cla/tac/h05010.htm.

know that it is he sitting at the right hand of Power and coming on the clouds of heaven (Matthew 26:63–65). But having rejected Jesus as Anointed, they refused to acknowledge *who* would acquire this empire, and thus *where* this transfer of power would take place. Notice that in Daniel, when Jesus comes on the clouds, he is not coming *to earth.* He is coming to the throne of God *in heaven.* That is where all rule is handed over to him. This is something that happened in the first century AD; the passages I've cited are unequivocal about this, and the historical record confirms it. Indeed, we can even have some confidence about the exact *timing* of this shift, since Luke's account of the Ascension is surely intended to evoke the language of Daniel 7:

> And when he had said these things, as they were looking on, he was lifted up, and a **cloud** took him out of their sight. And while they were gazing **into heaven** as he went, behold, two men stood by them in white robes, and said, "Men of Galilee, why do you stand looking **into heaven?** This Jesus, who was taken up from you **into heaven,** will come in the same way as you saw him go **into heaven."** (Acts 1:9–11)

Luke rather labors the point that Jesus went *into heaven*—on a cloud, no less. Given that his work of redemption was complete at this point, and he had given all the instructions to the disciples that he needed to, this is surely the moment at which he went to the right hand of God—which Daniel 7:13–14 and Psalm 110:1 are speaking of. And Peter directly references Psalm 110:1 shortly afterward at Pentecost, claiming that it has been fulfilled as he explains to the Jews what has happened (Acts 2:34–35). This theme is self-consciously completed in Acts 7, as Stephen is being executed:

> And he said, "Behold, I see the heavens opened, and
> the Son of Man standing at the right hand of God."
> (Acts 7:56)

This transfer of power from the gods to Jesus also notably spans about a generation, from the Ascension in AD 30 to the destruction of Jerusalem in AD 70 (*cf.* Matthew 24:34 etc). The imminence of this event is why, in Mark 1:15, Jesus comes preaching that "the time is fulfilled; the kingdom of God is *at hand.*" His point is that the kingdom of God is imminent; it is in the process of arriving through him. The fourth kingdom of Daniel is certainly Rome, and not Greece: it was Rome that executed Jesus, and it was Rome that held power when Jesus took over rulership of the nations. His kingdom *has now come.*

There is, of course, a future time when that kingdom will be consummated—fully established on earth at his second coming. We know, for instance, that sinners *will not* inherit that kingdom—a future event (*e.g.* Ephesians 5:5). But the very same kingdom has *already* unquestionably been inaugurated. Luke 17:20–21:

> Being asked by the Pharisees when the kingdom of
> God would come, he answered them, "The kingdom of
> God is not coming in ways that can be observed, nor
> will they say, 'Look, here it is!' or 'There!' for behold,
> the kingdom of God is in the midst of you."

Although the kingdom of God will *ultimately* come in ways that are very observable—no one is going to miss Jesus' return—Jesus is responding to the Pharisees' mistaken notion that it would come in their lives by military conquest. No, he says, but rather the kingdom is indeed already in this life, in the midst of them. It is exemplified in the very presence of Jesus, its king, and of his disciples, its people and viceroys.

Which brings us to a natural followup question which turns out to have far-reaching implications for preaching the gospel: *how* is God retaking Adam's kingdom from Satan?

# CHAPTER 6
## HOW GOD IS RETAKING ADAM'S KINGDOM FROM SATAN

*God used the collapse of his kingdom Israel, and the death of his king Jesus on a cross, to overcome sin and make the human nature itself sacred space. He thereby disarmed Satan's claim over humanity by crowning a perfect human king in his place—and started inexorably transforming Adam's ruined kingdom into Jesus' restored one by dwelling in human hearts instead of in a land.*

In Acts 8:12, Philip preaches the good news about the kingdom of God, and the name of Jesus the Anointed. Here, as in the synoptics, the gospel is about the kingdom, and about the man marked out by God as its king: Jesus. This is a significant contrast to the evangelical gospel preached today, which is a gospel of atonement. Although the atonement is critical *to* the gospel, it is not *itself* the gospel, and I don't know of anywhere in the New Testament that the gospel is either preached or summarized as such. I'll talk more about this soon; for now, I mention it in passing. The point I want to focus on here is not the content of the gospel, but the events which accompanied its preaching.

In Acts 8:7 we learn that the gospel message was accompanied by:

1. Unclean spirits being cast out;
2. Many paralyzed and lame people being healed.

In the same way, we read in Luke 9:1–2 (par. Matthew 10:1, 5–8) that Jesus "called the twelve together and gave them power and authority over all demons and to cure diseases, and he sent them out to proclaim the kingdom of God and to heal."

Notice the interesting parallelism here. He gives them authority over demons and to heal, and then sends them out to *proclaim the kingdom* and to heal. It is almost like Luke is rhyming the two phrases, so casting out demons becomes virtually synonymous with proclaiming the kingdom.

Why would that be?

## EXORCISM AS ANNEXING KINGDOM TERRITORY

I think the answer is quite obvious. Demons represent the worst of Satan's occupying force in Adam's kingdom. They are his footsoldiers, keeping a thumb on the human beings he rules. Demons are a clear and unmistakable sign that Satan is in charge—that this territory belongs to him. So casting them out *literally is* the same as proclaiming, or demonstrating, or proving, that the kingdom of God is at hand. It is an obvious, unambiguous way for people to see that God is taking back Satan's territory for himself. That he has, in the words of Colossians 1:13, "delivered us from the domain of darkness and transferred us to the kingdom of his beloved Son."

We see in this that the kingdom is not abstract. It is not that we have merely had our names moved from one column in a database to another; that God has added us to the kingdom in the sense that he has reserved us a seat for later. Membership in the present kingdom is not merely forensic; a pure legal declaration or a promise of a future reality. It is, in fact, a *present* reality which awaits a future consummation. A genuine change has taken place. We have moved from one kingdom to another in a *cosmological* sense: we have a new present ruler; we are his people; we are his territory. This is what the gospel is *all about.* "If I expel demons by the Spirit of God, then the kingdom of God has come upon you" (Matthew 12:28).

The movement of people from one kingdom to the other is how the gospel's power is manifested. And this cosmological change is not merely covenantal or relational; it is also ontological—wherein the true genius lies.

This requires some explanation:

## HOW THE KINGDOM OF GOD MANIFESTS TODAY

We know that a kingdom has a king, a people, and a territory. The king of the domain of darkness is Satan; its people are those who have not believed the gospel; its territory is everywhere those people live—but it is a *disputed* territory. Indeed, it is a territory over which Jesus has all legal claim—we have seen this already in the fulfillment of Daniel 7:13–14 and Psalm 110:1, and shortly I will explain the mechanism by which this works. For now, note that Satan still *possesses* much of that territory (pun somewhat intended), and he may therefore still exercise *power* in it—but his *claim* to it has been superseded by the second Adam.

That is bad, bad news for him, because without a legal claim, all he has is occupation by force—and as it turns out, he lacks the firepower required to prevent the gospel from spreading. Every time the Spirit of Jesus regenerates a heart, Satan's territory gets a little smaller.

Jesus is fulfilling Psalm 82 right now. He has been fulfilling it for two thousand years; he will continue to fulfill it until he comes again; and he will complete its fulfillment on that day. God has already sentenced the corrupt gods, and he is now busy inheriting their nations. When he is done, he will execute the final judgment on them, and all those who follow them, in the lake of fire.

It started at the cross, for as Jesus said shortly before he was crucified, "Now is the judgment of this world! Now the ruler of this world will be thrown out!" (John 12:13) How? Colossians 2:15 tells us that God disarmed Satan and the other gods, and put them to open shame, by triumphing over them in the cross.

And this gets us to the heart of the genius of God's redemptive plan, in which he combines the three elements of kingdom together in Christians themselves: a king, a territory, and a people...

## 1. A KING

The problem since the fall has been that men, by nature, cannot represent God. In our natural state we are *enemies* of God; we stalwartly refuse to rule on his behalf; we will always choose to rule for ourselves instead. We choose injustice over justice, vice over virtue, divisiveness over *shalom*, the greatness of our names over the greatness of his—because every thought and inclination of our hearts is only, always, toward evil; *i.e.*, away from Goodness (Genesis 6:5; 8:21; Jeremiah 17:9).

For God to restore Adam's kingdom, to make it his own kingdom again, he needed to find a loyal human viceroy to rule on his behalf. Someone who, in the words of Jesus, would do nothing on his own authority, but only speak and do what the Father gave him to do, in a manner pleasing to him (*e.g.* John 5:19; 8:28–29). But since the human nature is corrupted and defiled, it does not—and indeed cannot—submit to God's law (Romans 8:7). The only way for God to find a human ruler who would perfectly represent him...was for him to *become* that ruler.

This is what the incarnation was all about—and why the rulers in the heavenly places were so eager to execute Jesus. By killing God's perfect human king, they thought they would bring his plans of reclaiming and restoring the human kingdom to a swift end. But they hadn't thought it through...

## 2. A TERRITORY

You hopefully recall that the worship of God took place in sacred space: land that was set apart for, and inhabited by the pure, life-giving God. As one got closer to God, the space became more sacred—we've seen that in the divisions within the temple. But Israel itself was also sacred space. That's why there are the *kherem* commands when they enter the land: Joshua devotes certain tribes to complete destruction, at least in part because some were descendants of the Nephilim, the seed of Satan (*e.g.* Joshua 11:21–22). They therefore threatened God's own seed and defiled the sacred space of Israel. In the same way, many of the more puzzling laws around uncleanness were intended to maintain this sacred space, to keep it pure and free of any hint of death or aberration which would pollute it, contaminate it, violate it. Once again, this is physical imaging of spiritual realities: the ritual uncleanness was a covenantal representation of the real problem: the moral pollution it symbolized. If you wanted to remain part of the sacred people, to live in the sacred space—and especially to worship in the temple—you had to image the purity and holiness of God. Doing so didn't make you *morally* pure; only God himself could do that, through your faith (Psalm 32; Romans 4:5–8), and ultimately through glorification (2 Corinthians 3:18; 2 Peter 1:4; 1 John 3:2). But it did make you *representationally* pure. Ritual cleanness ensured you were "in good standing" with God, not morally, but in respect of the terms he had established for dwelling with and worshiping him.

The problem is, by our very nature we are *separated* from God by moral uncleanness. Because of our sin, we *cannot* come into sacred space (*e.g.* Psalm 5:4–5; *cf.* Habakkuk 1:13). We are forever excluded from God's presence. Israel's purity laws ultimately did not *make* anyone actually sacred, nor underwrite their approach to God—the Levitical cultus rather imaged how unapproachable God was because his people were *not* sacred; while simultaneously illustrating his great condescension in overlooking their sin and not destroying them. To be in good standing with God through ritual cleanness was an outrageous act of grace, where God condescended to treat a symbol of something grotesquely *false* as if the reality it represented were true—despite the moral depravity that utterly precluded being in good standing with him at all.

But for God to keep overlooking sin in this way requires a covenantal basis (*cf.* Romans 3:25). The covenant with Adam demands our death for disloyalty; God cannot overturn that by fiat without being lawless and untrue to himself (*cf.* Genesis 2:17; Hebrews 6:18 etc). The ritual purity laws didn't provide any covenantal basis for forgiveness, let alone moral restoration; they in no sense turned aside the force of the curse or repaired our total depravity. To allow us into sacred space—into the territory of his kingdom in other words—God had to make our moral defilement as nothing. He had to actually provide a way to reunite us to him. He had to find a way to *undo death.* Justice demands separation from his goodness, and punishment under his wrath. Citizenship in his kingdom is the very opposite of this, and thus demands changed hearts that love him loyally, rather than our natural hearts which hate him treacherously. The exact *problem* is that we only merit being cast from his presence into the darkness outside the walls of his kingdom (*e.g.* Matthew 8:11–12), and we cannot become loyal citizens.

How is this to be solved? How can God avoid eventually enforcing the curse of the covenant against everyone? How can he make Death itself, as Aslan puts it, start working backwards?

## 3. A PEOPLE

It is in the cross of Jesus that our separation from God is finally collapsed. This is what the rulers in the heavenly places had not thought through:

The very mechanism by which they hoped to end God's kingdom was the *consequence* of being excluded from it. The death by which they sought to destroy God's Son was the effect of *renouncing* sonship. The suffering by which they intended to destroy the faithful man was the curse for *breaking faith.*

But how could God be excluded from his own kingdom? How could he be separated from himself? How could Jesus not be the faithful Son? He could never merit death; John 1:4 tells us that Jesus has life in himself. So when the one who is life takes death into himself, what happens? Well, Paul would say that "death is swallowed up" (1 Corinthians 15:55). The problem of our fallen natures continually violating the sacred space of God, of the dishonored being incompatible with the glorified, of the perishable not mixing with the imperishable—the problem of sin, in other words, that ultimately led to God disinheriting the nations and exiling Israel—is dealt with ingeniously by *God himself* becoming perishable, being cursed as dishonored, of suffering in himself the consequence of a fallen nature, of being made sin.

God extends himself into the human nature itself, by taking on the form of a man in his Son, Jesus. He then allows his enemies to unknowingly create a covenantal contradiction. He allows Jesus to suffer the penalty of sin, treating him as if he himself were morally defiled, cursed, and cut off from God. But because Jesus is the one man who is *not* morally defiled—he is indeed infinitely more powerful than the power of sin, infinitely more pure than we are impure—this separation, this death cannot hold him (Acts 2:24). It is as if he is wrapped up in it, and because he is a holy fire, it simply burns up, turns to dust, and falls away.

Jesus is therefore vindicated by the Spirit as *not* cursed; he is raised from the dead as proof that God will not permit him to be cut off (1 Timothy 3:16; *cf.* Romans 1:4). The resurrection is the Father testifying, as Pilate put it, "I can find no guilt in this man" (Luke 23:4; *cf.* Acts 13:28–30). Having been vindicated from the curse of the law, the law now has no hold on him (Galatians 2:19–20). The requirement of the covenant is fulfilled and done away with. Death itself works backwards.

This would be bad enough for the wicked gods, because it means there is a perfect human ruler with a perfect claim to authority over Adam's kingdom. Their delegated authority is superseded by his. The only reason they were given any authority in the first place was because of man's failure. Now that there is a man who has not failed to represent God, who has remained a faithful son, they are done. Even worse, because that man is Yahweh himself, who has all authority, he has not only taken away their right to rule, but he has put them in *subjection* to a human being! Thus Adam's kingdom is no longer under the authority of Satan and his angels; it is under God and man. Power has changed hands: the kingdom of Satan that belonged to Adam has become the kingdom of God that belongs to Jesus—at least in terms of legal claim.

If that were the extent of it, the situation would be bad enough for the gods—but not especially promising for *us*. Fortunately, the gospel is not about them; God is not interested in taking back his kingdom from the gods if it contains only one man—even if that man is Jesus. He is interested in establishing a kingdom of *billions*; a great multitude that no one can number, from every tribe and language and people (Revelation 7:9).

The *real* problem for the gods, and the truly good news for us, is that a king's representation works upward *and* downward. We are made to represent God (upward); but he also represents us (downward). A human king stands in the place of his people before God— and he also stands in the place of God before his people. Indeed, this priestly function was typical in the ancient world; because of the nature of representation, kings were typically also priests. For instance, in Egypt, one of Pharaoh's titles was "High Priest of Every Temple."[1] Caesar was *pontifex maximus*, "greatest priest." Although God wisely separated these functions in the administration of Israel, they are merged again, and indeed *ex-*

---

1. Joshua J. Mark, "Pharaoh" in *Ancient History Encyclopedia:* http://www.ancient.eu/pharaoh/.

*emplified,* in Jesus—and in Melchizedek before him (Hebrews 6:20; 7:1; *cf.* 1 Peter 2:9).

Because of this representation, Adam, as the viceroy of God, stands in for all his descendants. Every person is naturally, covenantally identified with him—we are "in Adam" and so we are counted guilty before God (1 Corinthians 15:22 etc). By the same token, Jesus, God's new human king, stands in the place of any member of God's kingdom. Every person born of the Spirit is supernaturally, covenantally identified with him—we are "in him" and so we share in everything he has (Ephesians 2:4–6 etc). This includes his standing before God—we are counted righteous. But it includes far more besides, so that our fallen nature itself is undone and we become partakers of the divine nature itself (2 Peter 1:4). Because he has suffered the penalty of sin, the legal demand against anyone he represents is nullified. God looks to our representative to satisfy the demands of justice against us—*which he has.* But the true genius of the gospel goes further. It is found in this partaking of Jesus. This is how God brings us into his kingdom—by bringing his kingdom into us. Look at how kingship, territory, and people become merged after the cross:

## CHRISTIANS AS GOD'S KINGDOM

When God dealt with the defilement of human nature on the cross, he did not make any and all sinners undefiled. He did not undo the curse universally. He did not make human beings in general immortal and sinless. Rather, he made the human nature imperishable *in Jesus.* It is the man Jesus who was raised imperishable. It is the man Jesus who had all things put in subjection to him (1 Corinthians 15:27). It is the man Jesus who became a life-giving spirit (1 Corinthians 15:45). The human nature is made sacred *in Jesus.*

The mystery of the incarnation establishes an *ontological* connection between the human nature and the divine nature. Jesus is the greater temple (John 2:21) because God resides in a human body: that body is itself sacred space in a profoundly developed and fulfilled sense. It is somehow the physical location of the presence of God, no longer just in a mysterious representative way, but in an even more mysterious ontological way—God takes upon himself the nature of man (Philippians 2:8). And since all people share this human nature, all people may *in principle* now share in God's nature also. We can do this not by becoming God in the way that Jesus became man, but rather by having Jesus' divine nature *extended* to us; by being joined to him in such a deep and intimate way that he becomes part of our very beings. We cannot be represented by him, we cannot become imperishable like him, unless we partake of him. If we wish to have life in ourselves, we have to take life into ourselves—and the life is the Son. This is what the bread of life discourse in John 6 is all about.

It is also why Paul says that we have the "mind of Anointed" (1 Corinthians 2:16): it is the Spirit of Anointed which we have received (v. 12). He is joined to us in some inexplicable way when we are born again (John 3:3–8).

And this in turn is why Paul describes us as temples of the Holy Spirit (1 Corinthians 6:19). The physical temple has passed away because the spiritual archetype in Jesus has come. He was the reality which the temple had imaged—and because we are in him as he is in the Father (John 17:20–23), *we* become mini-temples ourselves. Or, to vary the metaphor slightly, we are "living stones" (1 Peter 2:5) building up the true temple, and indeed the true city of God, the New Jerusalem, which the physical Jerusalem pointed to.

We ourselves are sacred space. Wherever we go, we are walking on holy ground. Our very presence sanctifies the earth, through God in us. No wonder Paul can speak of the spouses of believers being made holy (1 Corinthians 7:14). We are not merely made faithful sons and loyal citizens of God's kingdom through rebirth and regeneration—we are made dwelling places of God himself (Ephesians 2:22), and so we become his *territory* also. This is how Jesus becomes our king.

> We *are* God's kingdom: by joining himself to us through the Spirit of Jesus, he makes our bodies his territory, changes our hearts to be loyal people, and dwells with us as our king.

And this is why Paul writes in Ephesians 6:12 that "our struggle is not against blood and flesh, but against the rulers, against the authorities, against the world rulers of this present darkness, against the spiritual forces of wickedness in the heavenly places." Since every Christian is literally a little piece of God's kingdom, wherever we go we are a threat to Satan's rule. It is our job to annex more pieces of his kingdom for God, through preaching the gospel—"for the weapons of our warfare are not of the flesh but have divine power to destroy strongholds. We destroy arguments and every lofty opinion raised against the knowledge of God, and take every thought captive to obey Anointed" (2 Corinthians 10:4–5).

---

Although somewhat tangential to the point I'm making, there is a crucial aside I must make here—if not for the sake of completeness, then certainly for the sake of candor. There is a significant interplay between the concept of believers-as-kingdom, and soteriology more generally, which has implications that you are best warned of in advance. The view I'm articulating here is grounded in the idea that we are identified with and participate in Jesus. If this sounds correct, that's because it is—but you will discover at some point that it rubs against the grain of much Reformed thinking as regards how imputation works for justification. Although I am not a Federal Visionist by any stretch, FV theologian Rich Lusk is not wrong when he notes that, while the idea behind imputation is certainly true, the transfer itself is not of *works* between *people*, but of *people* between *rulers or kingdoms* (Colossians 1:13–14).[2] It's fine to speak of imputation, but the devil is in the details—and there is an increasingly broad and obdurate stream of Reformed theology (of which I suspect John Owen is the fountainhead) which bungles how it works. Imputation per se does not make us right with God; union and subsequent identification with Jesus do. I agree with Lusk's contention that, following the likes of Luther, Calvin and Edwards, we should speak far less of *imputation* (a forensic category), and far more of *incorporation* (a covenantal and organic category). Jesus' righteousness—or more accurately, the verdict pronounced on him in the resurrection—becomes ours not by legal transfer, but by covenantal union. This includes a legal/forensic component, but much else besides.[3] If you find yourself agreeing with me on this, you should prepare yourself in advance to also find previously enjoyable theological discussions becoming awkward, and previously cordial Reformed fellows shunning you for "denying" *sola fide* and limited atonement. Better to know now.

---

## HEALING AS INAUGURATED ESCHATOLOGY

This brings us full circle to the two signs I noted as being indicative of the gospel going forth: exorcism and healing. If we are temples of the Holy Spirit, and if we ourselves are sacred space—the very kingdom of God on earth—then that explains why these particular signs always accompany the gospel, even today. When you read accounts of missionaries, it's always these two things: demons being cast out, and people being healed.

They are not unconnected. As I've said, the demons have to go because they are not welcome in the kingdom of God—as it expands in this present age, the demons' own kingdom shrinks by comparison. And sickness itself, like so many other physical things, im-

2. Rich Lusk, "A reply to 'The OPC Justification Report' on union and imputation" (June 2006), 7: http://www.federal-vision.com/pdf/lusk1.pdf.

3. For a more detailed exploration of imputation and justification, see D. Bnonn Tennant, "On the atonement, part 1: headship and imputation" (December 2008/July 2016): https://bnonn.com/on-the-atonement-1/ and "Faith Across Time: Is Final Justification Unchristian?" (February 2018): https://bnonn.com/final-justification-unchristian/.

ages a spiritual reality. It represents the power and bondage of sin. It is a precursor to death, which is what you get when sin is fully grown (James 1:15). Since the kingdom of God is defined by the presence of the Holy Spirit, and the Spirit gives life (Job 33:4; John 6:63; 2 Corinthians 3:6), so as bondage to sin in the spiritual realm is overturned through exorcism, it is also confirmed by the sign of healing.

The point is to show in the physical person what is happening in the spiritual arena. The physical healing is not resurrection, because the kingdom is not yet complete. It is, rather, inaugurated eschatology. The kingdom is already and not yet; ushered in but not fully realized; started but not finished; inaugurated but not consummated. So healing is a taste of what is to come. The resurrection of life from the dead is what will herald in the eternal kingdom, so it is fitting for the kingdom in this present age to be heralded by a lesser but similar sign. People are restored to health, in anticipation of being restored to life in the coming age.

This should also give us confidence to pray for healing within the *established* kingdom. If the Spirit is really active among us, then healing is hardly too difficult for him. Indeed, healing is a natural effect of his presence! Not that he will *always* heal; but certainly we should *hope* for him to heal. We simply have to...

> ...ask in faith, with no doubting, for the one who doubts is like a wave of the sea that is driven and tossed by the wind. For that person must not suppose that he will receive anything from the Lord; he is a double-minded man, unstable in all his ways. (James 1:6–8)

Unfortunately, when you don't have to rely fully on God, you often end up doubting him. When you aren't continually, intensely needing him, when you don't feel utterly helpless without him, you end up doubting him. So I've read accounts of Western missionaries who could not cast out demons, yet the local converts could.[4] The West has sapped us of a robust, dependent faith in the supernatural power of God. Just as Western missionaries can't cast out demons overseas because it all seems so remote and abstract to them, I think most of us lack the confidence in God's power to ask for healing in the way we should. Medical technology has made us spiritually dull, because so often prayer seems redundant: "You don't need prayer; you need a doctor." Medical technology is certainly a great blessing, but because we are so used to seeing healing happen in mundane, scientific ways, we have lost confidence in it happening in remarkable, supernatural ways.

If we want the kingdom of God to stand firm in the West, one of the things we must do is work to overcome our culturally-induced dullness. We must work to truly depend on and have faith in the power of God through his Spirit. We must not become crazy Pentecostals. But we must regain our vigor and our boldness in trusting our God to work powerfully. The Spirit of God is mighty to work—when we don't try to make ourselves mighty, and end up doubting him.[5]

This wraps up the arc of redemptive history into the present, but brings us to a new issue. We've seen how the kingdom of man was ruined by Adam, how it was refused at Babel, and how it is now being reclaimed by Jesus. But what about the future? What will the restoration and renovation look like, and how is it to be achieved? This is the last, and most important

---

4. See John Livingston Nevius, *Demon possession and allied themes: being an inductive study of phenomena of our own times* (F. H. Revell, 1894): https://archive.org/details/demonpossessiona00nevi/page/n5.

5. For a lengthy proof of this fact in the modern day, see Craig S. Keener, *Miracles: The Credibility of the New Testament Accounts* (Baker Academic, 2011).

question—because answering it reveals the very hope to which we have been called, which in turn informs the very gospel which we preach. And it is a gospel which doesn't resemble the modern evangelical gospel quite as closely as one may wish.

# CHAPTER 7

# WHERE WE ARE NOW, AND WHAT WE CAN LOOK FORWARD TO

*God's end-game is a human kingdom that is not just restored, but glorified, with believers taking their place as new sons of God, ruling with Jesus forever.*

I've argued that Psalm 82 is an anchor-point in redemptive history. It draws together the arc of God's kingdom in a very helpful way. Returning to it now, we've learned enough to explain more fully what I mean:

We have learned that God has begun executing the sentence against the gods of this world, but he has not yet completed it. The ruler of the earth has been stripped of his authority over Adam's kingdom by the second Adam, the perfect ruler and son, who flawlessly represents God because he is not just made *in* the image of God, but *is* the image of God—the exact imprint of his nature (Hebrews 1:3).

He has stripped Satan of his *authority,* but not of his *power*—yet. He has done what is necessary to finally depose the serpent and the other corrupt sons of God—and he has begun to take back the nations from them. Their power is weakened, and will ultimately be brought to nothing. But that final judgment has not yet happened, and so they still have some power over the world even as God is annexing it from them.

This is why we see Paul, for instance, saying that the gospel is "veiled to those who are perishing, because in their case the god of this world has blinded the minds of the unbelievers, to keep them from seeing the light of the gospel of the glory of Anointed" (2 Corinthians 4:3–4). Similarly he says we "were dead in the trespasses and sins in which we once walked, following the course of this world, following the prince of the power of the air, the spirit that is now at work in the sons of disobedience" (Ephesians 2:1–2). But then what happened to us?

> God, being rich in mercy, because of his great love with which he loved us, and we being dead in trespasses, he made us alive together with Anointed (by grace you are saved), and raised us together and seated us together in the heavenly places *[literally? No—]* in Anointed Jesus *[—he is in the heavenly places]*, in order that he might show in the coming ages the surpassing riches of his grace in kindness upon us in Anointed Jesus. (Ephesians 2:4–7)

Perhaps reading this book has encouraged you not to gloss over phrases like "seated us in the heavenly places" any more. To understand what it means that God has done this, we only have to ask who we have seen in the heavenly places already.

It is the sons of God. His divine council.

Our future hope is thus truly remarkable, because the kingdom of God that we are inheriting—the kingdom that God is now establishing through us—is not just a kingdom in which we are citizens. It is a kingdom in which we are *kings*. Viceroys of Jesus. It is a kingdom in which we *replace* the sons of God as rulers of the world. Jesus represents us, but *we also represent him.*

We are rulers on his behalf, sons of his Father—which means that if we are truly representing him, doing his work, we have his authority: authority even over the gods. This is possible because we have his Spirit:

> For all who are led by the Spirit of God are **sons of God.** For you did not receive the spirit of slavery to fall back into fear, but you have received the Spirit of adoption as sons, by whom we cry, "Abba! Father!" The Spirit himself bears witness with our spirit that we are children of God, and if children, then heirs—heirs of God and fellow heirs with Anointed, provided we suffer with him in order that we may also be glorified with him. (Romans 8:14–17)

We have been reborn into God's family. We have become Jesus' siblings. And if Jesus is the king of kings with all power and all authority given to him, we are part of the royal family. We are God's dynasty. Look at Revelation 2:26–28:

> The one who conquers and who keeps my works until the end, to him I will give authority over the nations, and he will rule them with a rod of iron, as when earthen pots are broken in pieces, even as I myself have received authority from my Father. And I will give him the morning star. (Revelation 2:26–28)

The use of the term *morning star* is obviously suggestive—but the main point is this: Jesus is adopting a new royal family right out from under the noses of the previous royal family who ruled us...and there is nothing they can do.

That is what Psalm 82 is pointing us to—and that is why the Holy Spirit inspired it. He didn't add it to the songbook of Israel because he wanted us to know about a one-time indictment of divine beings—something basically irrelevant to the history of human redemption. He inspired it because it is ultimately about us.

🔑 Psalm 82 is in our Bibles because it is a *turning point* in human redemption: a touchpoint for the gospel itself.

It is a promise that the evil rulership of the nations will not continue forever, but that it will be dealt with and replaced by the rulership of God. That is the whole purpose of the Psalm: it is messianic (v. 8)—imploring God to rise up and to execute his judgment against the gods by taking back the nations that they rule. The consequence of him doing this is what the gospel—the good news of the *kingdom*—is all about.

But this does not revolve around "heaven." The endgame is not us being together with Jesus in an ephemeral spiritual state when we die. To borrow the colloquial caricature, the gospel is not about how to get our own cloud, harp, and wings. The hope to which we are called is far greater, and quite honestly far more outrageous, in at least three ways:

## 1. HEAVEN WILL BE PHYSICAL

This may sound like a contradiction in terms—since God is spirit, surely heaven is a spiritual (read: disembodied) place. This is true with respect to what we see in most of the Bible; but when it comes to the eternal kingdom we find that heaven and earth merge: the dwelling-place of God becomes a physical, embodied state on earth, permeated by his Spirit. This is perhaps clearest in Revelation 21, where we see the new heavens and the new *earth*—with the assembly of God's people coming down *out* of heaven to it (Revelation 21:2, 9–10), followed by God's declaration:

> Behold, the dwelling place of God is with man. He will dwell with them, and they will be his people, and God himself will be with them as their God. (Revelation 21:3)

Indeed, this is already partially fulfilled today, since we are temples of the Holy Spirit—but we see in the consummated kingdom that this is vastly amplified, both because the whole physical world is our *undisputed* territory, and because God dwells with us there physically in the person of Jesus. Although the imagery of the New Jerusalem is poetic, the reality it points to is real:

> No longer will there be anything accursed, but the throne of God and of the Lamb will be in it, and his servants will worship him. They will see his face, and his name will be on their foreheads. And night will be no more. They will need no light of lamp or sun, for the Lord God will be their light, and they will reign forever and ever. (Revelation 22:3–5)

So we are not simply waiting to be with Jesus in a disembodied state when we die. That state itself is merely a stopgap until we are resurrected to rule as his viceroys, in his very presence, on a new, restored earth. What this will be like I do not exactly know. I don't think John means for us to press his images into such literal use that the new earth will have no sun nor moon— that would require a different universe with different laws of physics, and seems to obviously miss the point. The world as it is now will be "made new" (Revelation 21:5), not destroyed and recreated as an entirely different fantasy-world. As the old world was once cleansed in water, so the present one will be cleansed in fire (2 Peter 3:7)—not as an utter annihilation, but as a destruction of the wicked; a burning clean; a fresh start.

Presumably this fire encompasses—and is perhaps limited to—the second death; the lake prepared for the devil and his angels. Peter certainly intimates as such with his description of the "heavenly bodies" burning as the heavens pass away with a roar (2 Peter 3:10). It hardly seems fair to his intelligence to imagine that he doesn't have Isaiah 34:2–4 (*cf.* Isaiah 24:21–23) in mind:

> For the anger of Yahweh is against all the nations,
> and his wrath against all their armies;
> he has devoted them to destruction, has given
> them over for slaughter.
> Their slain shall be cast out,
> and the stench of their corpses shall rise;
> the mountains shall flow with their blood.
> **All the armies of heaven shall rot away,**
> and the skies shall roll up like a scroll.
> All their armies shall wither,
> as leaves wither from the vine,
> like leaves withering from the fig tree. (Isaiah 34:2–4)

That being so, the sun and the moon in Revelation are surely the same spiritual beings we've seen in Deuteronomy 4:19—not the physical astronomical bodies.

Although the world will not be annihilated, it will be renewed; and how much more, then, our bodies, which are united to God through his Spirit. Paul says that our lowly bodies will be transformed to be like Jesus' glorious one (Philippians 3:21): our physical form in the resurrection will be as superior to our current form as an oak is superior to an acorn (1 Corinthians 15:42–49). John agrees that "what we will be has not yet appeared; but we know that when he appears we shall be like him" (1 John 3:2). Becoming "partakers in the divine nature"

(2 Peter 1:4; *cf.* Ephesians 5:31–32) has significant consequences, not just for our spiritual state, but for our physical state also—because the physical images the spiritual. What exactly those consequences will look like is not explained—nor, I imagine, would we understand them if they were. We presumably lack the conceptual faculties to comprehend an eternal weight of glory beyond all comparison (2 Corinthians 4:17).

## 2. WE WILL BE MEMBERS OF GOD'S FAMILY-COUNCIL

As I've already mentioned, we will not merely be *citizens* of God's kingdom in glorious embodiment; we shall be his royal family—and because we represent him faithfully, having been freed from the bondage of sin, we have the right to reign with him (2 Timothy 2:12). Once again, the Bible does not provide details on the mechanics nor the logistics of this; but it does show that partaking of the divine nature elevates us above the gods we were created lower than (1 Corinthians 6:3; *cf.* Psalm 8:5; Hebrews 2:7). Since we are heirs with Jesus, we are the new sons of God; since we are *in* Jesus, we have been put over every ruler in the heavenly places (Ephesians 1:21; *cf.* Luke 20:35–36).

Without wishing to speak ill of anyone, I find it hard to overemphasize the importance of this, given how the gospel is typically preached today. Most Christians either don't consider, or merely pay lip-service to being sons of the King—without really considering that sons of the King will be called upon to *rule*. Having a clear understanding of the divine council, and how we replace it, brings both grave import and great awe to our calling as Christians. I will explicate the significance of this in more detail shortly.

### 3. JESUS HAS AN INHERITANCE TOO

Even more outrageously, the thing underpinning all this is not, ultimately, that Jesus is *our* reward and inheritance; it is that we are *his*. It is this single-minded divine affection, this unbreakable dedication to onetogetherness with his holy ones, that the whole history of redemption is built on. This is the joy to which Jesus himself looked as he contemplated the cross—and what was on the other side of it (Hebrews 12:2; *cf.* Isaiah 53:10–12; 65:19). Neither death nor life, nor angels nor rulers, nor things present nor things to come, nor powers nor anything whatsoever can separate us from the love of God in Anointed Jesus our Lord. All praise be to God for his unresting, unceasing, unchanging, unrelenting *chesed!*[1]

So he will certainly continue to adopt a family to himself, a great multitude as an inheritance and a reward, from every tribe and language and nation, until such time as he returns to complete his judgment of the earth. Then he will finally depose the gods of this world, he will secure his inheritance exactly as Psalm 82 says, and he will renew the earth to physically rule it with the new sons of God—us.

---

Understanding this as the endpoint of redemptive history adds an intriguing double meaning to Genesis 15:5; 26:4 when we remember that the host of heaven is also a great multitude, and that we are offspring of Abraham by faith (Galatians 3:7; *cf.* John 8:39–44). We tend to think of the stars of heaven as purely stellar objects, but surely Yahweh is here obliquely alluding to how he is one day going to replace the divine council with a human one.[2] He is saying, in effect, "your descendants will be like gods" (*cf.* Genesis 3:5 for some biting irony).

---

1. Lovingkindness or steadfast love; the covenant loyalty and affection God shows to his people, and which they in turn are to show to him.

2. This is the topic of an interesting series by David Burnett, who argues that the qualitative reading of Genesis 26:4 is well-attested in Second Temple literature. See David Burnett, "Paul's Use of Genesis 15:5 in Romans 4:18 in Light of Early Jewish Deification Traditions" (2017): http://drmsh.com/category/david-burnett-post/.

In short, Psalm 82 is a lens for redemptive history—through it we see the the problem of the rulership in the heavenly places, and how God is superseding that rulership with his own.

This returns us to the thesis that I started with: that the Bible views the spread of the gospel as God's transforming of Adam's kingdom, ruled by Satan, into his own kingdom, ruled by Jesus—a spiritual territory of restored human hearts, no longer separated from God by rebellion, but rather annexed from their previous rulers by God himself to dwell and govern there.

We can now see clearly how this works—at least in the biblical-theological sense. We can see how the gospel sits at the peak of the trajectory of the history of redemption—if you will forgive me so many ofs in one sentence. But this still leaves a lot of questions, the most notable of which have to do with our own role in bringing about this renewed world. What are the practical implications for us as Christians in the twenty-first century? What is the task God has given us to *do?* To answer this, we need to look first at the expectations contained in the gospel that the apostles preached, and secondly at our mission briefing given in the Great Commission itself.

# CHAPTER 8

# THE GOSPEL AS A MESSAGE OF TRIUMPH

*Whereas the apostles front-load the gospel with Jesus' resurrection for worldwide kingship, evangelicals front-load it with his death for sin. Thus, whereas the New Testament's gospel is a message about all-encompassing cosmic restoration through Jesus' resurrection and enthronement, today's gospel is a message about individual moral restoration through Jesus' death and atonement.*

At the risk of oversimplifying, or sounding contentious, or biting the hand that feeds me, I am going to start the final leg of this book with an explosive thesis:

The gospel of the New Testament is *cosmological*—and the Western world's moral crisis is a natural result of God's assembly failing to preach this gospel *as* cosmological, in favor of preaching it as merely *moralistic.*

**Note well:** I am using the term moralistic in its primary sense of "characterized by or displaying a concern with morality." I am not intending to connote its secondary—but colloquially popular—meaning of "Given to making moral judgments, especially in a self-right-eous or judgmental manner."[1] What I'm saying by describing the evangelical gospel as moralistic is that we treat it as being purely about dealing with the problem of sin. I am not impugning us as preaching a *different* gospel; I am only impugning us—or rather, the Lord rebuke us—for framing it in a way that is weak and lopsided compared to the apostles.

To explain what I mean, here is a composite of the *typical* evangelical gospel I've heard preached:

> You are a sinner, and completely unable to please God. Because God is just, he must punish sin—and so right now you are on your way to hell. But because he is also loving, he sent Jesus his Son to die in your place. He suffered God's wrath so that you don't have to. If you turn from your sin and believe in him, you will be forgiven and receive eternal life.

I have tried to give the strongest possible representation here, while still being true to what is *typical*. Many presentations are much weaker than this, but my concern is not with that—it is that even the strong presentations miss the mark. While there is much that is good and robust in this composite—nothing in it is *false*; heeding it will certainly be sufficient to accomplish what it promises—it is nonetheless fundamentally *skew*, because it is fundamentally *small*. This becomes clear when we compare it to the gospel preached in the New Testament:

- John the Baptist first announces the gospel by warning people to repent—to turn back to God—because the kingdom of heaven is imminent (Matthew 3:2).

---

1. "Moralistic" in *The American Heritage Dictionary of the English Language,* Fifth Edition (Houghton Mifflin Harcourt, 2011): https://www.thefreedictionary.com/moralistic.

- When Jesus begins to preach the gospel, he commands the people to turn to God, whose kingdom has now come on earth (Mark 1:14–15; Matthew 4:17, 23).

- After the cross, when Peter preaches the gospel at Pentecost, he traces the scriptural promises fulfilled in Jesus, and culminates in a message about how God has enthroned him as the king of kings, and is putting all his enemies under his feet (Acts 2:34–36). When the crowd reacts with consternation about how to make right their treason against God's chosen king, Peter tells them to turn back to God to have their sins blotted out (*cf.* Acts 3:19).

- When Paul preaches the gospel to the synagogue in Acts 13:16ff, his presentation follows a very similar structure: the first third is devoted to how God established a kingdom through Israel, through David—and how he has raised up Jesus as David's kingly descendant. Like John the Baptist and Jesus, Peter and Paul both front-load the gospel message with the kingdom of God, and with Jesus as its ruler and savior—a term we (not incorrectly) read through a salvific lens, but which in the language of the time was customarily used of kings and emperors.[2] Indeed, almost the entire discourse in Acts 13 is about Jesus and his worthiness to be king, proved by his being raised from the dead; it is only after establishing this that Paul goes on to briefly explain the personal application—namely, forgiveness of sins. Notably, he doesn't link forgiveness to Jesus' death at all; rather, to Jesus' right to rule—that is, his right to judge and to acquit. (I'll return to this later.)

---

2. "Saviour" in *Dictionary of Deities and Demons in the Bible,* Second Edition, eds. Karel van der Toorn et al (Wm. B. Eerdmans, 1999).

○ When Paul preaches the gospel to the Areopagus, he preaches Jesus as the judge of the world—*i.e.,* its ruler—and claims that God has proven this by raising him from the dead. He warns them that God now commands everyone to turn from their worthless gods to him (Acts 17:30–31).

---

Bear in mind that in pre-modern culture, trials by ordeal were a pervasive part of the administration of justice. You see this as late as the medieval period with trials by combat, and at least as early as the Exodus (prefigured by the Flood), with the Israelites crossing the Red Sea safely while the Egyptians were drowned. In the same way, when they crossed the Jordan on dry ground, the hearts of the Canaanite kings melted (Joshua 5:1), because they knew it meant that Yahweh had upheld Israel's claim on their land. To pass through a typically fatal ordeal—usually water or fire—was taken as a divine vindication of one's innocence (*cf.* Daniel 3:28–30; notice also the irony of v. 22). Thus Jesus' resurrection was a powerful testament that the charges against him were false, and that although man had found him guilty, God had found him righteous—overturning the previous verdict by repealing his death sentence after the fact. This also significantly factors into the breaking of Satan's legal right to accuse; *cf.* Romans 8:31–33; Colossians 2:14–15; Zechariah 3:1–2; Revelation 12:10.

---

○ In Romans 1, when Paul prefaces his treatise with a summary of the gospel, he includes these elements: (1) as promised in Scripture, (2) Jesus is God's Son, (3) descended from David according to the flesh; (4) was resurrected from the dead; (5) declared by the Holy Spirit to be in power (i.e., reigning); and (6) is now bringing about the obedience of faith among the nations. We could also add (7), as a kind of presupposition, that it achieves this through its power for salvation (Romans 1:16). Paul concludes Romans again with elements 1 and 6; presumably as a kind of paraliptic synecdoche—taking the first and last parts to stand in for the whole.

○ In 1 Corinthians 15, he describes many of the same elements as Romans 1: that Jesus died—this time adding "for sin"—was buried, was raised, all in accordance with the Scriptures, and then appeared to many witnesses (vv. 1–9). But here, the gospel summary is a setup to move into an extended description of what seems to be in Paul's mind its central theme: Jesus' current reign. To refute the heresy at Corinth, Paul elucidates the *hope* of the gospel, which is that everything will be made subject to Jesus the sovereign king; and that when this is finally completed, we will all be raised from the dead to live in his kingdom (vv. 20–28).

The fundamental element which is *always* explicit in these summaries of the gospel is that God has now established his kingdom. This is *why* the Greek word *euangelion*, which we translate as gospel, is used in the New Testament: the term had already acquired the technical meaning in classical Greek of a message of victory.[3] By the time of Jesus, the terms "gospel" and "savior" were used together commonly to refer to the (ostensibly) glad tidings of an emperor establishing his rule. A "gospel" was a message of triumph proclaimed on behalf of a "savior" who had brought order, harmony and healing by taking dominion upon his shoulders—what in Hebrew you might call a *sar shalom*, a prince of peace (*cf.* Isaiah 9:6; 60:1–2; Luke 4:16–21).

In the gospels themselves, this is primarily anticipatory; the message of the kingdom being established through the ministry of Jesus. After the cross, every time the gospel is summarized it is even more specific on this central point:

I. **God has now established his eternal kingdom through the vindicating resurrection of his chosen king, Jesus.**

Two other elements are also *always* implicit on the surface, and often completely explicit:

---

3. *The New International Dictionary of New Testament Theology,* Volume 2, ed. Colin Brown (Zondervan, 1976), 107.

2. Every person is required to turn to King Jesus from their previous loyalties to escape his judgment;

3. When we do, our sins will be blotted out and we will inherit eternal life in his kingdom.

We could quibble and say that the requirement to *believe* the gospel is a separate element also—but this seems confused to me. Obviously one must *believe* the message to act on it, but this is just a standard feature of any discourse, and so it is, as philosophers would say, trivially true and thus uninteresting.

The key point is that when the New Testament abbreviates the gospel *holistically*—unless I have missed some other place—it *always* does so by presenting Jesus as the risen and reigning king, and demanding a response to his impending judgment. It is then generally the *effect* of our response, and *because* of his kingly right to judge, that we receive and have confidence in our personal vindication before his Father. In Romans 1 and 1 Corinthians 15, justification—but also glorification—is presupposed as the *result* of the gospel rather than an element in its message; in Acts 2 and 17 it is omitted entirely, pending the audience's response; in Acts 13 it is a more central benefit of Jesus' kingship. Right standing with God, in other words, is the *result* of Jesus' triumph over every other power, and often is the *solution* that Peter and Paul offer only once their audiences have declared their loyalties—whether to Jesus, or whether to themselves and their gods.

Jesus' death receives even less focus. I'm not suggesting that the atonement doesn't underwrite our justification; obviously it does (*e.g.* Romans 5:9).[4] But I am

4. Indeed, aside from the emphasis I give the atonement in chapter 6, I have also written extensively on the theological and pastoral importance of getting our doctrine of

pointing out that in the Bible's own gospel summaries, our salvation is not framed within the rubric of Jesus' death for our justification. Jesus's death is not even always mentioned explicitly. It is only linked to atonement once (I Corinthians 15), and is half the time omitted entirely (Acts 17; Romans 1). Rather, it is the **resurrection** which receives focus. This is true sometimes even in more focused discussions of justification, because the resurrection is God's acquittal of Jesus through the overturning of his death sentence—which in turn is the basis for our own acquittal before him (*e.g.* Romans 4:25; I Corinthians 15:17).

So here's my worry:

> Whereas the apostles front-load the gospel with Jesus' resurrection for worldwide kingship, evangelicals front-load it with his death for sin. Thus, whereas the New Testament's gospel is a message about *all-encompassing, cosmic* restoration and renewal through Jesus' resurrection and enthronement, today's gospel is a message about *individual, moral* restoration through Jesus' death and atonement.

As I see it, we have somehow turned from preaching enthronement to preaching atonement. Now, as I've said, atonement for individual sin is *important.* Being declared holy, and becoming holy, are *important.* Indeed, the personal moral element of the gospel is *so* important that we have some kind of instruction about it in every book of the Bible. God certainly wants us to *be* his people, and that is only possible with personal moral restoration. But this personal moral element is not the core message of the gospel in any of the places it is summarized or preached holistically in the New Testament. If we take a focused discussion, like that in Galatians, of this one element—indeed, a focused discussion of one component of this one element, for justification and salvation are not synonyms—and then treat it as normative for the *whole* gospel without regard to how the apostles themselves summarized that gospel, we will certainly produce a distorted picture.

To understand the gospel as a holistic message, we need to look at the places where it is presented as such. To know what it is fundamentally about, we need to look at the places where this is explained most simply (*e.g.* Mark 1:14–15). Looking at the didactic parts of Scripture that zero in on some or other key *element* of the gospel is only fruitful once we have the whole picture in place—otherwise we'll end up extremely unbalanced.

Another way of getting at the problem is to ask the simple but nagging question that bothered me ever since I became a Christian: **where is the gospel in the Bible?** Is it plainly stated in the gospels? If not, why are they *called* gospels? Is it plainly stated in the Old Testament (with adjustments for that period of redemptive history)? If not, how could any Jew be expected to know it? And if they could not know it, how could they be saved?

But the fact is, the evangelical gospel is not stated plainly in the gospels. It is not stated plainly in the Torah. It is not even stated plainly, as such, in the epistles. It is an invisible gospel to anyone without the benefit of relatively modern systematic theology. A gospel which would have been veiled to Jews, to Gentiles, to the early church.

What, then, *is* the gospel? I have suggested that it is a message of triumph, but that is more a paraphrase of how I think we should translate the term *euangelion*.

The gospel, in its most basic sense, is **the message of who Yahweh is and what he has done,** so that every knee should bow and every tongue confess him as Lord. In the Old Testament, that is summarized in the ten commandments. "I am Yahweh your God who brought you out of the land of Egypt, out of the house of bondage." *That* is the gospel—which then produces the obedience of faith. *Who* God is bookends the ten commandments (Exodus 20:1–2, 18–21). The response required is the obedience of faith, summarized in verses 3–17.

In the New Testament, as I have already shown, the gospel is summarized in the message of who Jesus is and what he has done, which produces the same response of faith—not mere belief, but **loyal reliance.** Faith, when lived, looks like the ten commandments. It looks like obedience (Romans 1:5). It is passive in receiving Jesus (Romans 4:5), but active in abiding in Jesus (John 15:4–6; *cf.* 1 John 2:6). It is done *to* us in order to be done *by* us.

Another way of saying this is that the law/gospel distinction is not in the text, but in the reader. To the regenerate man, all Scripture is gospel (*cf.* Psalm 19:7); to the unregenerate man, all Scripture is law (2 Corinthians 2:14–16).[5]

So without diminishing the importance of Jesus' death, atonement, and justification of sinners, these are not the gospel. They are *elements in,* and *effects of* the gospel. The gospel *achieves* individual salvation: justification, sanctification, glorification—but only because of its whole object, Jesus the just, holy, glorious king of the *kosmos.* This relationship between the content of the

---

5. For an excellent summary, see Douglas Wilson, "Cold Law, Hot Gospel" on Blog & Mablog (April 2019): https://dougwils.com/the-church/s8-expository/cold-law-hot-gospel.html.

gospel (the kingdom and its King; Romans 1:1–6), and its subsequent effect (salvation; Romans 1:16), is clear throughout the New Testament. It is why, for example, Paul describes God as having "delivered us from the domain of darkness and transferred us to the kingdom of his beloved Son"—the gospel of the kingdom—"in whom we have redemption, the forgiveness of sins"—the *effect* of that gospel (Colossians 1:13–14). This redemption, this forgiveness of our sins, is subordinate to our being transferred from the kingdom of darkness to the kingdom of light, from the rulership of Satan to the rulership of Jesus. The gospel is the power of God for salvation *because* it is about God transferring us from a kingdom of death to a kingdom of eternal life.

Within the context of the kingdom theology I've articulated, then, the gospel is the triumphant message of God's vindication of his human king, to take back Adam's kingdom from both the gods and the guilt that previously enslaved us, and to restore the cosmos under his rule.

But this brings me to the 64 kilodollar question:

## WHY DOES IT MATTER?

My argument is essentially enthronement versus atonement. Again, speaking to what is typical—and varying theological streams finesse this with varying degrees of robustitude—the evangelical gospel is reduced from a cosmological message about Jesus' kingship, to a moralistic message about personal salvation. And personal salvation itself is typically framed in terms of Jesus' atonement for our justification, rather than in terms of our participating in his sonship.

This matters, not just because it isn't the right way to present the gospel, but because framing it this way has enormous follow-on effects—some of which you can probably already see given the kingdom theology I've articulated. A moralistic gospel *sees* less than a cosmological one. Because personal moral restoration is at the heart of the evangelical gospel, its vision naturally shrinks to the individual level. To prove this, let me simply ask how many evangelicals you know who have a clear view of at least the *broad strokes* of kingdom theology that I've canvassed in this book? They lack this view, not because the broad strokes are obscure, but because the way they think about the gospel effectively precludes it from being the peak of a redemptive-historical trajectory that involves *cosmic rule*. What they tend to see instead is a trajectory of individual salvation, drawn together perhaps in God's election of a corporate body. So, for instance:

- They see the world in John 3:16 as being all individuals, rather than a kingdom;

- They think of salvation in terms of going to heaven, rather than inheriting eternal life on a renewed earth;

- They think of their church as a club to be joined, rather than a household within God's kingdom, by which his family rules itself, and expands his rule in the world;

- They don't think about spiritual rulers at all, and certainly deny the existence of other gods.

But these are just minor symptoms compared to the major problems that arise. When we pare down the gospel until all that remains is the personal moral angle, we end up with a faith that *hopes* for less, that thus *demands* less, and therefore ultimately *achieves* less. To explain what I mean, we need to now turn to the Great Commission itself.

# CHAPTER 9

# THE GREAT COMMISSION AS A DIRECTIVE TO CONQUER

*The evangelical moralistic gospel hopes less, demands less, and achieves less than the all-encompassing ambitions of the New Testament's cosmological one. If Jesus really is ruling until he puts all his enemies under his feet, then he is creating a new nation out of all the old ones through the Great Commission—and this happens geometrically until there is nothing left for us to do.*

I have alleged that the evangelical gospel, being moralistic rather than cosmological, hopes for less, thus demands less, and therefore ultimately achieves less. This reflects my thesis that the Western cultural crisis is the natural consequence of preaching a moralistic gospel.

To begin to now illustrate what I mean, and how serious the ramifications are for every aspect of our effectiveness as God's viceroys, let me ask you a simple question:

What is our mission as Christians?

Any Christian can probably answer this—but the devil is in the details. How about this: *Our mission is to go and make disciples in all the nations, baptizing them in the name of the Father and of the Son and of the Holy Spirit.*

At first blush that seems right—but if you are paying close attention, you will notice that I have changed a word...and left out a bunch of others. This *isn't* quite what the original mission briefing actually said. The marching orders Jesus gave were more specific, and more detailed:

> All authority in heaven and on earth has been given to me. Therefore, go and make disciples **of** all the nations, immersing them in the name of the Father and of the Son and of the Holy Spirit, **teaching them to observe everything I have commanded you**—and behold, I am with you all the days, until the end of the age. (Matthew 28:18–20)

This commission is obviously for the congregation at large, given that the original disciples died well before the end of the age—as, no doubt, shall we. So this is not merely a general order; it is a *standing* order; and not merely *a* standing order, but *the* standing order—our Prime Directive. The Great Commission is General Order 1, as issued by the commander-in-chief of the kingdom of God. As such, while it is the task of the congregation's various leaders to direct those under them to enact this order, it is also the duty of every one of us to uphold it, promote it, and work towards its success.

But to do this, we need to understand exactly what it is we're upholding, promoting, and working towards. And therein lies a problem, given the evangelical gospel of personal moral restoration—personal belief in a personal savior.

As we've seen, the *full* gospel is the message that the kingdom of God is triumphing over the kingdom of Satan, because God has established a new king, Jesus, who as a perfect son is completely righteous and worthy to rule, and has therefore been given all authority in heaven and on earth. The rulers and authorities, the cosmic powers over this present darkness, the spiritual forces of evil in the heavenly places, are no longer in command; they are under God's anointed human king.

A key point here is that Jesus is *presently* ruling—all authority *has* been given to him, as he told the disciples in the original mission briefing. He *is* seated at the right hand of the Majesty on high (1 Peter 3:22; Hebrews 1:3; 12:2; Ephesians 1:20; Daniel 7:13–14).

But what is Jesus *doing* with this rule? Is he just waiting for individuals to invite him into their hearts? Is he holding his breath for people to accept the wonderful plan he has for their lives? Is he just chilling around up there, hoping for one of his children to finally advise the last unreached people-group about him, so the end can come (Matthew 24:14)?

Is he hanging tight until then, waiting for the time when he can establish his kingdom?

No. *Hell* no.

He is currently exercising his rule. He is right now establishing his kingdom. He is at this very moment reigning until he has put all his enemies under his feet (1 Corinthians 15:25; Psalm 110:1; Acts 2:34–35). I'm not talking about general providence. God has always reigned through general providence, and if that was all the gospel was saying, it wouldn't be very interesting. The Son of God was doing general providence before the cross, but he wasn't putting all his enemies under his feet.

No—Jesus is putting his enemies under his feet in the same way that *any* king does: by conquering through battle. It is his assembled people who assault the gates of hell (Matthew 16:17); it is his soldiers who engage in personal combat with the angels who oppose him (Ephesians 6:12–13); it is his army who sets up siege-works to tear down strongholds (2 Corinthians 10:5). He is, after all, not only a man of war himself (Exodus 15:3), but the Lord of hosts (1 Samuel 4:4; Exodus 12:41). Hosts means armies.

He is establishing his kingdom and putting every single one of his enemies under his feet *through his congregation*, through the Great Commission.

Christians are **representatives of the king**. We are, as it were, ambassadors with swords (*cf.* 2 Corinthians 5:20; Matthew 10:34). You cannot fail to notice, when reading the Great Commission, that it is *predicated* on Jesus' authority:

> All authority in heaven and on earth has been given to me. **Therefore**, go and make disciples of all the nations, immersing them...teaching them... (Matthew 28:18–20)

As commentators are quick to note, it is making disciples which is the main verb here: that is the action Jesus is commanding of us. In the Greek it is just one word. Translators are bafflingly reticent to take advantage of English's remarkable flexibility, but I am not, so allow me to whimsically translate our job as *disciplenating* the nations. The Great Commission is an analogy to and an extension of the original kingdom commission that God gave to his viceroys Adam and Noah (Genesis 1:28; 9:1): the task of carrying his name into the world, multiplying themselves, and ordering creation on his behalf. This is the very thing that we are called to do—and we achieve it by disciplenating the nations. **The Great**

**Commission is nothing less than an update to the dominion mandate.**

We fulfill this updated mandate in three ways: by going, by immersing, by teaching. Each of these is predicated on Jesus' authority: it is *because* he has been given all authority that we are to go, to immerse, to teach. Each is an exercise of authority on behalf of Jesus:

1. **We go** into enemy-occupied territory, commanding that everyone turn from their rebellion and bend the knee to our king (Acts 17:30–31), falling on his mercy (Acts 2:21), because it is *his* territory, and he will one day judge those who live there;

2. **We immerse** those who obey, as a public repudiation of their former wicked loyalties, and as a pledge of allegiance to, and identification with, the rightful king (1 Peter 3:21);[1]

3. **We teach** within the structure of the assembly, as our patriarchs exercise their authority to speak on behalf of the Patriarch of all (*cf.* Ephesians 3:15), to instruct, reprove, exhort, and train in righteousness unto full sonship, the obedience of faith (Romans 16:26; 2 Timothy 3:16–4:2).

But the striking thing I want to draw your attention to here is *who* we are supposed to do this with: **God's people are commanded to disciplenate all the *nations*.**

### THE MORALISTIC GOSPEL HOPES FOR LESS

In the Great Commission, Jesus does not say, "Go and disciplenate *in* all the nations." He does not say, "Go

---

1. For more on this concept, along with why I don't just use the normal Christianese term baptism, see Appendix 2: Baptism as a Pledge of Allegiance.

and disciplenate *citizens* of the nations." He does not say, "Go and bring disciples out *from* the nations." His explicit focus is the nations themselves: it is they, as corporate bodies *comprised of* and *ruled by* households and individuals, who are to be made disciples. The nations themselves are to be "trained for the kingdom of heaven"—to borrow the ESV's rendering from Matthew 13:52 of the same "disciplenate" lemma. This makes perfect sense—indeed, how else could we accomplish the dominion mandate? It would not *be* a dominion mandate if it did not involve actual dominion! The Great Commission is the unfolding fulfillment of Psalm 2, which speaks of how Yahweh laughs at the nations who rage and plot pointlessly against him. Why? Here is the reason it gives:

> I will tell the decree;
> Yahweh said to me: "You are my son;
>> today I have begotten you.
> Ask from me and **I will make the nations your heritage,** [*cf.* Psalm 82:8]
>> and your possession the ends of the earth.
> You will break them with an iron rod.
>> Like a potter's vessel you will shatter them."
> So then, O kings, be wise.
>> Be warned, O rulers of the earth.
> **Serve Yahweh with fear,**
>> and rejoice with trembling.
> Kiss the Son
>> lest he be angry and you perish on the way,
>> for his anger burns quickly.
> Blessed are all who take refuge in him. (Psalm 2:7–12)

Paul begins and ends the book of Romans by explicitly describing the gospel in the same way, saying that according to God's declaration of Jesus as the Son of God now in power—and its corollary of all the *other* sons of God as now *out* of power—it was Paul's task to bring about "the obedience of faith among all the nations" (Romans 1:4–5; 16:26; *cf.* Romans 15:18). These are his very first and very last words in Romans, summarizing the entire purpose of the gospel as bringing about this subservience (*cf.* 1 Peter 1:2).

Paul was aware of the promise in Psalm 86:8–10 that all the nations will come and bow down before the Lord and glorify his name. He was aware of the promise in Isaiah 11–12 that when the shoot came from the stump of Jesse, he would make the predatory nations lie down with God's lambs, and it would end with the earth being as full of the knowledge of Yahweh as the waters cover the sea (Isaiah 11:9). He was aware that Pentecost was the overt beginning of this process through the reversal of Babel: that just as God had broken down his kingdom by having the people hear different languages when they exalted their own name in their one tongue, so he had begun to rebuild his kingdom by having them hear one tongue when they exalted his name in their different languages (*cf.* Acts 2:21).[2] Pentecost publicly signaled his reinheritance of all peoples unto the obedience of fidelity, after his disinheritance of them for their disobedience of infidelity. This is surely why Paul went to such trouble to seek an audience with Caesar (Acts 25:11 etc); and why he instructed Timothy to pray specifically for kings and all those in authority (1 Timothy 2:1–4). Since Jesus has deposed the gods of the nations due to their corrupt rule, and since all dominion is now placed on him, so now all authorities must reform their rule to act as his proxies, and to represent his reign.

He is their king.

This is why Daniel 2:44 straightforwardly says that, when the God of heaven sets up the kingdom that shall

---

2. My thanks to Michael Foster for pointing out the importance of names in this reversal, in addition to tongues.

never be destroyed, it shall break in pieces all the other kingdoms and bring them to an end—it alone shall stand forever. Daniel 7 recapitulates this theme, describing the kingdom give to the Son of Man as follows:

> To him was given dominion
> and glory and a kingdom,
> **that all peoples, nations, and languages**
> **should serve him;**
> his dominion is an everlasting dominion,
> which shall not pass away,
> and his kingdom one
> that shall not be destroyed.
> And the kingdom and the dominion
> and the greatness of the kingdoms under the whole heaven
> **shall be given to the people of the holy ones of the Most High;**
> his kingdom shall be an everlasting kingdom,
> and **all dominions shall serve and obey him.**
> (Daniel 7:14, 27)

To put this in blunt, modern parlance, the cosmological gospel of the apostles is postmillennial. It expects Jesus to actually *put* all of his enemies beneath his feet before he returns to depose the final tyrant, death (1 Corinthians 15:25–26). It expects him to actually *establish* his kingdom at the expense of all others; to actually *destroy* all dominions opposed to him; to actually *reign* over all the nations by the time he is done.

It expects the yeast to actually leaven the whole lump (Matthew 13:33).

By and large, this is not the expectation of the evangelical gospel. By focusing on a message of personal moral restoration, and combined with the profound effect of Dispensationalism, it has abandoned the greater expectation of *cosmic* restoration in the present age. It does not expect it, so it does not hope for it. Because evangelicals treat the gospel as a personal entreaty to individuals to exercise personal faith, they end up with a *private* religion, practiced behind closed doors in the designated areas, and occasionally brought awkwardly into the public square for evangelism—but certainly never into the public *office*, which as we all know is secular. Christians aren't to represent Jesus as if he actually ruled their *nation*.

But as I've just canvassed, the gospel is inherently political. Doug Wilson observes that no one actually has the option of deciding between a theocracy and a more neutral political regime; theocracy is inescapable. There is always a god of the system. The question is not *whether* to have a god, but *which* one to have.[3]

## NOT OF THIS WORLD?

Although I understand Christians reacting negatively to the political abuses of Christianity in the past, I am frustrated by the vehemence of the common evangelical claim that Christianity has *nothing* to do with statecraft, since God's kingdom is "not of this world" (John 18:36). The fact that Jesus' kingdom is not *of* this world does not imply that it is not *on* this world.

The context of John 18:36 is Pilate's interrogation of Jesus with respect to the charges brought against him. When Jesus says that his kingdom is not of this world, he is emphasizing that he is not the kind of king Pilate is expecting; that he is not a king of a nation *within* the world; that his power is not derived *from* the world—remembering that *kosmos* in John typically refers to the fallen kingdom of Adam.

3. Douglas Wilson, "A Primer on Theocracies" on Blog & Mablog (January 2018): https://dougwils.com/books-and-culture/s7-engaging-the-culture/a-primer-on-theocracies.html

What Jesus cannot be saying is that his kingdom either does not exist on earth, or that it has nothing to do with rulership of the earth. Neither of these would make any sense whatsoever. The *telos* of the gospel is to fully establish God's kingdom *on earth* to the exclusion of all others—that is what we ask for in the Lord's Prayer (*cf.* Matthew 6:10)—and a kingdom by definition has not only a ruler, but a hierarchy of rule. The reason God's kingdom is not of this world is because it does not derive its power from the previous fallen dominion, rather imposing divine dominion *onto* the world through Jesus himself. Indeed, God's kingdom ultimately replaces the fallen dominion by *transforming* it (Revelation 11:15)—and this is inherently earth-bound.

But if the aim is for the gospel to transform the world so that Christians ultimately rule it with Jesus (*cf.* 2 Timothy 2:12 etc), then divorcing this from state-craft is incoherent. The *telos* of the gospel is inherently political in this respect, and a primary demand of the gospel is to bring us to competence for rulership in the eschaton. Regardless of how you think that cashes out in terms of millennialism, you can't simply divorce this key element of the gospel from the art of government, since it ultimately *is* the art of government.

I'm not going to stake out a position on how Christians should navigate politics, whether individually or as congregations. I'm simply pointing out that we *must* navigate politics, because a key element of the gospel is rulership of the world—and that *just is* political.


POSTMILLENNIALISM AND TRANSFORMATIONISM


Some people prefer the term *optimistic amillennialism* to *postmillennialism*, because they see the postmil view placing its eschatological hope in transformation of the world, rather than in Jesus' return.[4] While I agree that transformationism or triumphalism carries dangers, and must be attenuated against more pessimistic passages like Matthew 13:36–43 (which falls directly after Matthew 13:33) surely the difference here is only one of emphasis. Postmillennialism doesn't place its hope in the transformation of the world; it places its hope in Jesus' reign, which *brings about* the transformation of the world, and is *consummated* with his return. Creating yet another eschatological label hardly seems a good solution—especially since amillennialism technically refers to a view without any millennial reign, and sees the church age in terms of peaks and troughs that ultimately average out. As I have just argued, this is completely wrong. Thus I prefer the term postmillennialism—and if anyone asks for clarification, I will further say that the Bible depicts the regener*ate*, rather than regener*ation*, holding sway over all people by the time of the second coming.

## THE MORALISTIC GOSPEL DEMANDS LESS

Because it hopes only for personal faith, and for a government that will leave us in peace to practice it, the evangelical gospel is blind to the demand of Jesus that we disciplenate the nations—i.e., that we treat them as whole organisms, macro-scale households, and train their governments and their peoples in righteousness. Because the evangelical gospel doesn't place itself at the apex of the trajectory of Adam's kingdom, it doesn't see the Great Commission as the means of God's reinheri-

---

4. For an example of the supposed distinction between postmil and optamil, see the discussion in Vern Poythress, "2 Thessalonians 1 Supports Amillennialism," *The Journal of the Evangelical Theological Society* (37/4) (1995), 529–8: https://frame-poythress.org/2-thessalonians-1-supports-amillennialism/.

tance of the nations into a single kingdom, the household of faith, united by his rule. And because the evangelical gospel doesn't preach Jesus as the Son of God *now* in power, nor Christians as his family representatives, it cannot orient itself confidently against all the other sons of God striving to maintain power, nor their unwitting adopted representatives.

The gospel we hear today is rather a message about what Jesus has done for you—and how you can secure the benefits of that work. This is obviously not, in itself, unbiblical—yet nonetheless it fundamentally *reverses* the dynamic of power that the apostles preached:

> Whereas the apostles' gospel was a challenge for people to serve Jesus, the evangelical gospel is an offer for Jesus to serve people.

The means of securing Jesus' service is given as *belief.* In a strong presentation, this belief is couched in terms of trust, and is coupled with repentance. But because the focus is on personal moralism, the repentance is framed negatively, as a turning *from* sin, and the trust is framed in terms of the *atonement.*

Compare this to the response demanded by the apostles' cosmological gospel. Since Jesus is the enthroned king, the message is not primarily an offer to receive right standing before God, but rather a challenge to bow the knee to our rightful sovereign. Right standing—as with any king—is a benefit then conferred as a result of our fealty, and his own faithfulness. We give our loyal obedience completely to him, and rely on his own faithfulness to us in return. Right standing is thus placed in its proper context as the means by which he can declare us fit subjects of his kingdom—

the consummation of which is our salvation (*e.g.*, 1 Peter 1:5, 9, 13).

Put in Old Testament terms, it's a question of fidelity versus idolatry. It is a question of the *chesed* and *emet*, the loving loyalty and the being true, that underwrites all of God's dealings with his covenant people—and should underwrite their dealings with him. Repentance is not merely a turning from sin, but a turning *to God.* It is not a mere repudiation of sin, but a complete re-alignment of our reliance and our loyalty. Because we commit ourselves to Jesus as his subjects, yielding ourselves to him, and because we know that he has been given all power and authority, and because we know he has died for sin already, and because we know that his representation of us is not merely regal, but familial through rebirth and adoption into his family—because of all these things, **our confidence for salvation is a confidence primarily in *his right to vindicate us when he exercises his judgment as king.*** We know it is his atoning work that makes his declaration of our right standing true—but we would know that his declaration was true even if we didn't know *how,* as all God's people in the Old Testament did!

The moralistic gospel, by contrast, is not a demand to bow the knee to the one who can vindicate us as judge; it is an offer to believe in the one who died for us as sacrifice. Even in strong presentations that emphasize Jesus' lordship, we are still typically asked to place our confidence in the *atonement.*[5] As I noted in the previous chapter, this creates an extremely awkward kink

---

5. In the Owenic tradition of limited atonement the situation is even worse, because treating the atonement as the grounds of the gospel offer creates a vicious paradox where any confidence becomes completely impossible, and the gospel disappears entirely. See D. Bnonn Tennant, "On the atonement, part 2: the grounds for the universal gospel call" (December 2008/July 2016): https://bnonn.com/on-the-atonement-2/.

in what should be a straight line between Genesis 3 and Matthew 28: if you ask an evangelical teacher how Old Testament believers were saved, they will certainly affirm that it was by faith—but by faith in *what*? Well, they will say, by faith in God's promise of a coming redeemer. But that is manifestly untrue. To take just the starkest example, Naaman, a Syrian idolater of exceedingly dubious theological clarity, was right before God knowing neither a jot nor a tittle about the promised Anointed. The *only* thing he did right was this:

> "...from now on your servant will not offer burnt offerings, nor sacrifice to any god, but Yahweh." (2 Kings 5:17)

He makes this declaration as he is asking for soil to worship on—presumably thinking that Yahweh is confined to the land of Israel like any other god—and in the midst of admitting that he will continue to serve in the temple of a foreign god—so please could Elisha check with Yahweh that this is OK because Naaman doesn't really mean it! Yet Jesus contrasts Naaman's faith to the faithlessness of Capernaum (Luke 4:27).

Naaman goes in peace with Yahweh (2 Kings 5:19; *cf.* Romans 5:1) not because of his faith in a coming savior—for he has learned of no such savior, nor professed any such faith. The *only* thing he has done is give a pledge of allegiance to Yahweh.[6] His faith is not primarily a placing of belief in a promise, but rather a placing of loyalty and confidence in Yahweh himself as the cosmic king (v. 15). He has learned who Yahweh is, and seen what he has done—he has learned the gospel—and he responds accordingly. That is the demand of the cosmological gospel in the Old Testament (it is the first com-

---

6. See Appendix 2: Baptism as a Pledge of Allegiance.

mandment!) and it is *exactly the same demand* made in the New Testament. What does the thief on the cross say? "Remember me when you have finished making atonement?" No. "Remember me when you *come into your kingdom*" (Luke 23:42). He is expressing fealty to, and reliance on, the man he has recognized as the cosmic king.

In short, by making the gospel moralistic, we have robbed it of its power over the loyalties of all people everywhere (Acts 17:30). By focusing on what it can do for us, rather than on the response *demanded* of us as subjects of Jesus, the king of the world, we have forgotten to preach that he *is* the king of the world.

## THE MORALISTIC GOSPEL ACHIEVES LESS

The telos of the gospel is to fully establish God's kingdom on earth to the exclusion of all others, imposing divine dominion onto the world through Jesus via his people's representation. God's kingdom ultimately replaces John's *kosmos*. What Jesus is doing right now is creating a new nation out of all the old ones, to carry out his Great Commission (1 Peter 2:9)—and this happens geometrically until there is nothing left for us to do (Revelation 11:15).

The Great Commission is at the heart of this:

When we pray, "Your kingdom come and your will be done on earth as in heaven" (Matthew 6:10), this is not a pious nod to the eschaton. We aren't asking for the inevitable—that God would someday fulfill his long-term promise, as if he could fail in that regard. We are asking for God's intervention in the present. We are asking him to *help us fulfill the Great Commission and establish his kingdom on earth.*

Understood in the context of kingdom theology, this is a prayer for God's people to go out and overcome Satan and his angels, tear down their bases of power, and set up Jesus' rule there instead. It is a prayer for God to go out in our presence and fight with us by transforming Satan's territory into his own—that is, the territory of human hearts (*cf.* 2 Corinthians 2:14ff). It is, simply stated, a prayer to *conquer.*

God is certainly powerful to achieve this, but he will achieve it through the *cosmological* gospel he has given us: the challenge for all people everywhere to serve Jesus. He will not achieve it through the offer for Jesus to serve all people everywhere. It isn't that Jesus came not to serve (Matthew 20:28); rather, it is that even though for a short while he did make himself our servant, nonetheless he is now exalted as our king (Philippians 2:8–11; Hebrews 2:7–8). *We* are *his* slaves (*e.g.*, Titus 1:1). Thus, if we wish to achieve what the gospel promises, we must actually preach that gospel, as the apostles did.

The cosmological gospel preaches that Jesus is king over the world—including the Western world. It is the power of God for salvation for the same reason that it is the power of God for the obedience of faith among the nations. The moralistic gospel preaches personal moral restoration, which—if God is gracious—will achieve that end...but only that end. And as I will go on to argue, it is no longer even achieving that.

# CHAPTER 10

# THE URGENCY OF PREACHING JESUS AS KING OF THE WESTERN WORLD

*The results of the evangelical gospel are things like easy-believism, an inability to squash the Lordship Salvation controversy, moralistic therapeutic deism—and ultimately cultural relativism due to the privatization of religion. The New Testament's cosmological gospel confronts these errors.*

Jesus is, of course, the king of the *whole* world—but since I am an evangelical, and evangelicalism is a broadly Western phenomenon, my focus is Western.

I don't want to end this book on a downer; indeed, my purpose is to *encourage* evangelicals to reform how we preach the gospel, because the gospel is glorious. But to really drive home the *need* for this, we have to consider where the gospel of personal moral restoration has led us.

## PRIVATE, ME-CENTERED RELIGION

Since the focus is personal moral restoration—starting with Jesus' service to us rather than our service to him—the evangelical gospel has naturally produced all kinds of me-centered errors, glibly summarized in the trite catchphrase, "Christianity is not a religion, it's a relationship." These errors started in the assembly, of course, but because culture is downstream from religion they have certainly not stayed there.

This principle, that culture is downstream from religion, is important for seeing the implications of how we preach the gospel. Culture is the whole gamut of activities, expressions, and institutions of a *kingdom.* Activities, expressions and institutions always reflect prior ideological or religious commitments: a kingdom in which the predominant commitment of men's souls is to the flesh rather than the Spirit produces a culture like Hollywood; a kingdom in which the predominant attitude to God's fatherhood is hatred produces a culture of feminism; etc. So to say that culture is downstream from religion is simply to say that out of the abundance of the heart the mouth speaks, and the body acts—and that this happens at a corporate level as well as at a personal one. It is really just another way of saying that every society is theocratic.

This is why I think we can trace plausible connections between the evangelical gospel and many of the cultural-religious phenomena that now beset us. Every gospel, true or false, if believed and lived out, will produce fruit in keeping with its heart. The fruit produced in society—the society, indeed, that it produces—reveals this gospel at its root. So let me mention just a few of our own cultural fruits to demonstrate the urgency of restoring the cosmological center to our gospel. I'll start with the bad and move on to the badder:

## OPTIONAL CHURCH MEMBERSHIP

This might seem an odd place to start, but it jumps out to me for various reasons. A Christian who doesn't see his place in the assembly of God's people as a place in a *dynasty*—a ruling household regulated by a hierarchy of authority—will tend to treat his local congregation like a social club. Church becomes a group of like-minded people who meet together regularly to enjoy their mutual interest; membership becomes a handy way to have one's say in how the club is run, but is hardly *necessary* for being involved. By the same token, a congregation that doesn't see itself as a local limb of a cosmic body that organizes and represents God's authority on earth will fall into exactly the same trap.

But a Christian who defines his identity in terms of kingdom will naturally ask what the place of the local congregation is in that kingdom—and what his place is in the local congregation. By the same token, a congregation which thinks the same way will naturally see itself as a household, a microcosm of the greater house of God. It will therefore not teach believers to *join* it, for this would be redundant, even incoherent: they are *already* joined to it by merit of being born into it from above. Rather, they are to *submit* themselves to the adoption that God has done (*cf.* Hebrews 13:17; Romans 11:17), finding their place and purpose in the family. A local assembly is not a club; it is a body and a tree and a household; the organ by which Jesus grafts in and structures and knits together his people, the society in which he disciples them (Matthew 16:18–19), and the instrument by which he then disciplenates the nations.

Following Jonathan Leeman, it has become popular—in my circles at least—to liken a church to an embassy.[1] But while this is an improvement on the typical model of a social club, it is not the image that Scripture itself uses. The embassy image still reflects a fundamentally *individualistic* and *legal* understanding of

---

1. Jonathan Leeman, *Church Membership: How the World Knows Who Represents Jesus* (Crossway, 2012).

God's kingdom; Scripture reflects a fundamentally *organic* and *familial* understanding of it. The endemic Western failure to appreciate this has deep and varied roots which I am not competent to explore; I would tentatively point, at least, to an unbalanced emphasis on the forensic nature of justification in the Reformation, and even more to the industrial revolution, which led to the obliteration of our knowledge that the household is the basic society from which all other societies grow.

This may seem like an oddly ancillary point, but it is actually so foundational that I expect my next book to be about recovering the household as the key to a *practical* return to the cosmic gospel.[2] For now, suffice to say that Scripture depicts us as representatives of God because we are *sons* of God (*cf.* John 5:19–20). As sons of God, we build up the *household* of God (*cf.* Ephesians 2:19; 1 Timothy 3:15). Church membership is therefore not a way to exercise voting rights, nor a method by which a congregation can separate the confessionalists from the non-confessionalists. It is simply how the household of God recognizes, relates to, works with, and governs its own family members.

## EASY-BELIEVISM

This is rampant in less robust evangelicalism, for the obvious reason that Jesus is frequently presented as being desperate to save us regardless of what we do—rather than ready to spit us out of his mouth should we fail to work out our salvation with fear and trembling (*cf.* Revelation 3:16; Philippians 2:12).

---

2. That said, Chris Wiley has done most of this work for me; see C.R. Wiley, *The Household and the War for the Cosmos: Recovering a Christian Vision for the Family,* Canon Press (June 2019).

The downplaying of a changed life is a natural consequence of seeing faith as belief rather than fealty; its object as the atonement rather than our king; its purpose as therapeutic rather than covenantal; its outcome as placation rather than adoption and vindication.

The beast of easy-believism has many boastful heads. Within more conservative or Reformed congregations, another of these heads rears up in the form of an odd antinomianism, where faith and works are fully declutched, and a kind of phobia takes grip at the notion that, as Turretin put it, "good works are required as the means and way for possessing salvation"[3] (John 8:31; 14:19–21; 15:4–7; Galatians 6:7–8; Colossians 2:6; Philippians 3:12; 1 John 2:28; 3:24; Hebrews 12:14; Revelation 21:27 etc). This is again a natural consequence of a gospel that leads with justification through believing in the atonement, rather than a gospel that leads with Jesus' kingship, then lines up *all* salvific benefits behind adoptive union with him.[4]

## THE LORDSHIP SALVATION CONTROVERSY

That this was able to ignite in the first place is surely a testament that evangelicals do not see salvation as a benefit of Jesus' all-encompassing kingship. Worse, we have not even refined our gospel comprehension in the fires of this controversy.

An anecdote to illustrate: I once had a discussion with a solid, Reformed preacher—a pastor for decades—as to whether Jesus' lordship is vital to salva-

3. Francis Turretin, *Institutes of Elenctic Theology,* Volume II (17.3.3).

4. For a slightly different angle on the same issue, see D. Bnonn Tennant, "Works-righteousness: a square contractual peg in a round covenantal hole" (March 2018): https://bnonn.com/works-righteousness-a-square-contractual-peg-in-a-round-covenantal-hole/.

tion. He mused that, although it surely is, explaining *why* is not so easy.

But would anyone say this who understands the gospel as preached by the apostles? Jesus' lordship *just is* that gospel! If he is not your king, then you are not a citizen of his kingdom; in which case you certainly won't inherit it. If he is not your head, then you are not a member of his body. If you are not adopted under the authority of his Father, then you are not his brother.

I wish to speak no ill whatsoever of this father in the faith, whose labor for the Lord far exceeds my own. But when I explained the logic above, he was nonplussed. He knew intuitively that Jesus is our savior *because* he is our lord, but he could not put his finger on why. Given the difficulty that evangelicalism has had in dealing with Lordship Salvation, he cannot be alone. If such a well-trained man doesn't grok the gospel of the apostles, what hope is there?

## MORALISTIC THERAPEUTIC DEISM

This is the term coined by sociologist Christian Smith to describe the religion of the West—especially the religion of millennials. It is a worldview in which God exists; watches over the world; wants us to be nice to each other as we pursue happiness so we can go to heaven when we die; and is there for us when we need him.[5] Rather than involving transformative revelation from God, as Collin Hansen puts it, religion has thus become a utility for enhancing one's life.[6]


5. "Moralistic therapeutic deism" on Wikipedia: https://www.wikiwand.com/en/Moralistic_therapeutic_deism.

6. Collin Hansen, "Death By Deism" in *Christianity Today* (April 2009): http://www.christianitytoday.com/ct/2009/aprilweb-only/116-11.0.html.

Evangelicals have been writing about this for years. Albert Mohler, for example, wrote in 2009:

> Clearly, millions of our neighbors believe that moralism is our message. Nothing less than the boldest preaching of the Gospel will suffice to correct this impression and to lead sinners to salvation in Christ.[7]

It's as sad as it is ironic that Mohler accurately identifies neither the root of why so many people think our gospel is moralism, nor the correct solution. His suggestion is effectively to double down; to shore up the slip of the moralistic gospel into therapeutic deism by just preaching harder. Is it any surprise that our neighbors think our gospel is about personal moral improvement when that is what we consistently preach? Yes, no doubt they have misunderstood the work of Jesus in it. But they have certainly gotten the hang of the broad strokes. Can there be any serious doubt that the wholesale replacement of the true gospel with moralistic therapeutic deism is not directly connected to the evangelical moralistic gospel? And can there be any serious doubt that continuing to preach that gospel as the solution will do anything except produce more of the same problem—and worse, as we now see the SBC, ERLC and others predictably slide into heretical wokeness?

## CULTURAL RELATIVISM AND PRIVATE RELIGION

The natural evolution from easy-believism to moralistic therapeutic deism finds its endpoint in the complete relativism of the modern progressive movement. This includes progressive Christians, and the secular left,

---

7. Albert Mohler, "Why Moralism Is Not the Gospel—And Why So Many Christians Think It Is" (September 2009): http://www.albertmohler.com/2009/09/03/why-moralism-is-not-the-gospel-and-why-so-many-christians-think-it-is.

but has sadly come to characterize a large swath of evangelicalism as well.[8]

This is the polar opposite to apostolic Christianity. At the evangelical end, a sharp wedge is inserted between theology and politics, to the point that the very existence of such a thing as political theology is functionally denied.[9] Faithful Christians are lambasted by pundits for abdicating the moral high ground in their voting—as if the desire to move the nation's laws closer to God's, rather than further from them, were inherently dirty. The Christian witness thus becomes reduced to virtue-signaling.[10] This in turn enables the progressive and secular extremists, so the wedge goes deeper, and the gap between gospel and culture continues to widen. God, if he exists at all, now exists to serve and affirm us—we make the rules, we define reality, we take the place of God. Thus: feminism, abortion, identity politics, same-sex mirage, #lovewins, women are men, pets are children, yada yada yada.

However, the *key* problem to note here is **totalitolerance.**[11] *Because* the end result of the evangelical gospel's lopsidedness is man placing himself over God, the one

8. For a representative demonstration, see Toby Sumpter, "Keller's Baal Problem" on CrossPolitic (January 2018): http://crosspolitic.com/kellers-baal-problem/. Keller is just a prominent example of a widespread phenomenon that intersects with the culture of celebrity in evangelicalism.

9. Thomas Bradstreet, "The Sorry State of Evangelical Political Theology" on Sovereign Nations (March 2018): https://sovereignnations.com/2018/03/28/sorry-state-evangelical-political-theology/

10. For an excellent dissection of modern evangelicals' complete abdication of the task of disciplenating their nation—to the point where they are now entirely dependent on the corruptness of the state for their own "moral witness"—see Stephen Wolfe, "The Role of the State in Evangelical Moral Witness" on Sovereign Nations (May 2018): https://sovereignnations.com/2018/05/15/state-evangelical-moral-witness/, where he observes that "Respectable evangelical politics is facilitated by the State, is dependent on the State, and gets its greatest moral witness by reacting to the necessary actions of the State. Gospel-driven politics is state-dependent moralizing."

11. Douglas Wilson, "Totalitolerance" on Blog & Mablog (August 2015): https://dougwils.com/books-and-culture/s7-engaging-the-culture/totalitolerance.html.

kind of speech that becomes anathema is exactly the kind we are called to—the kind that places God over man. When God's household fails to disciple the nations unto the obedience of faith (Romans 1:5), the nations in turn ensure that we cannot later renege. So the heart of the moralistic gospel's failure is that it ends in a complete reversal of our prophetic place in the world:

> Rather than God's people schooling those still under Satan's power, and bringing them into submission to Jesus, the world is now schooling *us*, and bringing us into submission to Satan.

Thus we are left with Inverted Christianity (iChristianity). Our faith becomes relegated to private religion—if we're lucky. Blasphemy laws turn turtle, are renamed to hate speech, and smother Christian expression. I have experienced this iChristianity first-hand; for instance, with the correlation between the moralistic gospel and the defense of homosexuality. Since God loves everyone, and Jesus died for everyone, Inverted Christians infer that God accepts everyone. Indeed, since God is love, and sodomy is love, sodomy is godly. The only things that *aren't* godly are judgment, offending people with terms like *sodomy*, and averring that God still has commandments that only children of Satan avoid keeping (1 John 3:10).

A few representative comments from iChristians I've spoken to may help drive home the remarkable urgency of the problem (original typos faithfully preserved):[12]

12. D. Bnonn Tennant, "This is what we're up against" (June 2015): https://bnonn.com/this-is-what-were-up-against; all emphases and sloppy writing original.

as Christian's we know it's wrong because that's what the bible says. But God did not grant us the right to judge others that's for him only. Also we don't have the right to condemn homosexuals for their sins when we are not perfect ourselves.

god loves all his children unconditionally. Who are we to say what's evil or not? Marina Martinez [a pro-gay commenter] does not "approve of sin". Thats pretty disrespectful and your assumptions make you look like a christian extremist. You can quote the bible all you want, bur at the end of the day, all you are is a sinner. Like all of us. God gave us free will. Leave those people to it. Its not YOUR PLACE to tell people what they can or can't do, or how they live their lives.

I'm a very christian person. Being a Christian does not mean that you cannot rejoice in the happiness of others. On Sunday, our pastor made sure that the first thing he said in church was, "Let us rejoice over the acceptance of our neighbors! Love Wins!" Jesus condemned no one. In fact, he opted to spend his time with those who felt like they were outcasts. It is not our job to judge anyone. It is our job to recognize love where it shows itself. It is our job to be happy for those who can finally be free. Leave the judgment up to God, and love everyone around you. "Be like Jesus" does not mean that we can pretend to have the same power that he does. "Be like Jesus simply means to spread love, happiness, and acceptance to those around you.

In the same vein, a correspondent on my blog shared his discovery that the handbook for MOPS, an international church outreach program, explicitly directs its leaders to "keep Christian talk to a minimum" for fear of offending the very mothers they're trying to share Christianity with.[13]

13. See https://bnonn.com/baptism-as-a-pledge-of-allegiance/#comment-38500.

The problem of God's kingdom reversing its role with the nations isn't new; as I've suggested, the moralistic gospel has its roots in the Reformation and the industrial revolution. We've been failing notably in our task as God's people since at least universal suffrage. There are also other complicating factors, such as the bridal mysticism movement even earlier than that. But in the 20th and 21st centuries the problem accelerated. For instance, God's people in Germany failed monstrously on this point in the early 1930s—and that had a lot to do with Hitler cunningly turning their Two Kingdoms theology against them.[14] But I don't think he would have been *able* to do that if German Christians had stuck to General Order 1 (Matthew 28:18–20) and maintained a clear-eyed view of their role as *disciplers* of their nation on behalf of Jesus, the king over Hitler. The same is true of the assembly today with respect to feminism, socialism, and social justice causes.

Perhaps another way of summarizing what's going on here is that **a purely moralistic gospel teaches us not to fear God.** Because it is couched in terms of God loving us, and Jesus dying for us, it causes complacency. Yes, in robust presentations, repentance *is* preached, hell *is* preached, fleeing the wrath to come *is* preached. But *within* the assembly, once we accept the gospel, we are inclined to stop fearing God.

I am not talking about abject, craven terror *à la* medieval Papism. I am talking about the beginning of wisdom (Proverbs 9:10). As Adam Young reputedly put it,

If you stop fearing the Lord, you will stop fearing sin. And when that happens, everything you deem unthinkable suddenly becomes tolerable, passable, admirable, moral, legal, and even applaudable.

When you stop fearing the Lord, the only thing that becomes unthinkable is upsetting man. When you stop fearing the Lord, you cannot image him.[15] Then cow-

14. Though he is ironically deep into the apostate social justice movement now, see Joel McDurmon, "Horton's inglorious 'two kingdoms' theology" on American Vision (January 2013): https://americanvision.org/6882/ho-two-kingdoms-always-turns-out-radical/.

15. For further discussion of this principle as it applies especially to young men, see D. Bnonn Tennant, "You can't image God if you don't fear him" on It's Good To Be A Man (March 2019): https://itsgoodtobeaman.com/you-cant-image-god-if-you-dont-fear-him/.

ardice replaces boldness, and niceness inevitably replaces love. Inverted Christians who fear man preach God's wuv, rather than God's judgment. The Great Commission transmogrifies into showing how *nice* iChristianity makes people, in the hope that others will want to join the club. Witnessing becomes twisted from testifying about their king, to testifying about how accepting they are—just as accepting as the world. And when iChristians have finally perfected fitting into the world, so the world will accept iChristianity, the world asks why it *needs* iChristianity, and the iChristians are left speechless.

Thus the gospel of personal moral restoration rots on the vine.

Inverted Christians are of utterly no use in carrying out the Great Commission.[16] Indeed, they are the opposite of useful, because the only time their spines work is when they are tearing down the *actual* Christians—condemning them as extremists who give Jesus a bad name through preaching his coming judgment and associating him with intolerance and bigotry.

On this point, the evangelical gospel has dovetailed perfectly with the ongoing feminization of the church that started in medieval bridal mysticism, and blossomed under feminism. Because feminine discourse tends toward comity, our abandoning of the dynastic hierarchy that God built into creation and commanded of his congregation—namely, the rule of fathers—has predictably created a vicious cycle in conjunction with the evangelical gospel. God's people are tripping over themselves in a race to the bottom, to see who can be first and best in being nice to unbelievers, while simul-

16. For a good example, see Mike S. Adams, "Onward Christian Pansies" on Townhall (July 2016): https://townhall.com/columnists/mikeadams/2016/07/08/onward-christian-pansies-n2189346.

taneously silencing the voices within that threaten to disrupt this false peace by calling for the congregation to exert a command presence in the world.[17]

The rot eats through God's kingdom until it is ineffective against Satan's. Culture is downstream from religion.

## THE COSMOLOGICAL GOSPEL CONFRONTS THESE ERRORS

Would the gospel of Jesus' kingship overturn all these errors in an instant? Even if it were *believed* it would not fix the problems of evangelicalism overnight. But it would certainly move us in the right direction. Neither would it be immune from distortion and error itself— for instance, I can imagine prosperity teachers and the signs-and-wonders brigade happily incorporating kingdom theology into their abominations. Indeed, dominion theology is halfway there.

But at least we would be starting from the right foundation in correcting them. At the risk of laboring the point, I'm confident that you can see from the examples I've given that preaching the cosmological gospel directly confronts the seeping errors of evangelicalism—and replaces its wet noodle with a real backbone for the Christian witness in the culture at large.

I don't mean to suggest that I have discovered something the entire evangelical world has overlooked. Most of what I have said in this book I learned from others, and although I have not seen the elements pieced together in quite this way before, the broad strokes are

17. For another entrypoint to this problem, see D. Bnonn Tennant, "Calvinism, masculinity and niceness" (September 2016): https://bnonn.com/calvinism-masculinity-niceness/.

being painted elsewhere.[18] Nor do I suppose that I have articulated the Bible's kingdom theology with complete balance or accuracy or comprehensiveness. I am not a full-time theologian, and my perspective and study is limited.

Nevertheless, this understanding of the kingdom of God is not widely disseminated in evangelicalism—and I am convinced that it *needs* to be. Although each point taken individually could be considered a relatively unimportant item of trivia, collectively they build a biblical theology that *matters*. The very message and power of the gospel rests upon it. As I have argued, the failure of the modern church in the West is directly connected to the moralistic gospel it preaches. If we want to bring about the obedience of faith in our own nations, we must restore the cosmological center to the gospel. We must preach it as a message of triumph. We must preach Jesus as King.

18. One example with respect to recovering cosmic kingship—though he doesn't use that exact term—is Matthew W. Bates, *Salvation by Allegiance Alone: Rethinking Faith, Works, and the Gospel of Jesus the King* (Baker Academic, 2017). See also Scot McKnight's "King Jesus Gospel" (http://www.christianitytoday.com/edstetzer/2012/february/king-jesus-gospel-conversation-with-scot-mcknight.html), and N.T. Wright's *The Day the Revolution Began*. It does concern me, however, that so much of this work is being done by scholars compromised by the cult of the academy and the idolatry of Athens (*cf.* Acts 17:21). We need many more orthodox pastors and lay teachers in faithful Reformed congregations to be developing this kind of biblical theology.

# BUT POLYTHEISM! AND OTHER ASSORTED CONCERNS

*In which I defend divine council theology from a litany of well-worn but misplaced objections that you will either have thunk up yourself, or will encounter soon enough.*

From experience, I can tell you that Christians have three responses when they learn about the divine council in Scripture. Curiously, there is no reliable way to predict which response you will get ahead of time:

1.  **Complete apathy.** No matter how you draw out the implications of rulership in the heavenly places for the arc of redemptive history and the preaching of the gospel, they just shrug and say, "Oh ar."

2.  **Complete enthusiasm.** You barely need to explain the broadest strokes of what is happening in Deuteronomy 32 or Psalm 82 or Colossians 2—why all the 2s I ask?—and they are wondering how no one told them this before and why they failed to spot it all these years.

3.  **Complete loathing.** Every exegetical fallacy and every logical contortion will be meticulously explored as a refuge from this novel, false, distracting, false, divisive,

false, foolish, false, ear-tickling, false, liberal, and ultimately false doctrine.

I don't pretend to understand the first response, and I *really* don't understand the third—especially since it isn't indexed to any particular theological position or aptitude. Nonetheless, among more biblically literate evangelical opponents who fall into this third camp, you will encounter some flavor of each objection outlined below.

## 1. THE DIVINE COUNCIL IS HENOTHEISTIC

This is the foreboding charge that Richard Pierce, president of James White's Alpha & Omega Ministries, brings against Mike Heiser—and anyone who thinks his description and defense of divine council theology makes sense.[1]

If you believe that God created mighty spiritual beings, with whom he consults (as per 2 Chronicles 18:18–22), to whom he delegates authority over earthly affairs (as per Job 1:6–12; Psalm 82:1–2, ESV), and under whom he placed the rebellious nations after Babel (as per Deuteronomy 32:8–9, LXX & DSS)...does that make you a henotheist?

The only reason to even ask the question seems to be as a strategy of rhetorical mischief akin to a leftist suggesting that Christians are homophobes. It's a scurrilous use of language calculated to refute by association, rather than by argumentation. In the case of the

---

1. This accusation was made on Facebook, in a post originally accessible at https://www.facebook.com/richard.c.pierce.3/posts/ 1104619386222031?comment_id=1104886162862020. Unfortunately I did not think to archive this URL before I was summarily banned for making the arguments outlined here, and the post itself was shortly afterward removed. Heiser is hardly the only evangelical scholar to accept the divine council doctrine, but he has certainly done the most work to popularize and defend it.

divine council theory, if you will permit me to mix my metaphors, it is a case of building a strawman to poison the well.

## THE ROCK AND THE HARD PLACE

Basically, the divine council opponent has two options here:

### i. Define henotheism properly

In this case, henotheism is the transitionary point between polytheism and monotheism, in the supposed evolution of religion invented around the turn of the nineteenth century by liberal text critics like Friedrich Wilhelm Joseph von Schelling. It *permits* worship of other gods—at least within a given pantheon of ontologically similar deities—but *reserves* worship for a particular god who is considered supreme.

Obviously formal henotheism is a flagrant mischaracterization of the divine council view. Yahweh is not a member of a pantheon, and he is not ontologically similar to other deities. Rather, there is a council of mostly unnamed gods who are contingent beings created by Yahweh, and over whom he rules as the transcendent, uncreated "I Am." Moreover, all faithful (or simply well-informed) Christians reject the concept of religious evolution inherent in henotheism, whether they believe in the divine council or not.

### ii. Define henotheism really broadly

On the other hand, one can say that henotheism is simply a general affirmation of other deities in some broad sense. But then it loses *all* its rhetorical force—for if henotheism merely requires a basic affirmation of the existence of other gods, then Christianity is henotheistic *even if you reject the divine council view.* The New Testament itself explicitly upholds the existence of at least one other deity than Yahweh:

> And even if our gospel is veiled, it is veiled to those who are perishing. In their case **the god of this world** has blinded the minds of the unbelievers, to keep them from seeing the light of the gospel of the glory of Anointed, who is the image of God. (2 Corinthians 4:3–4; *cf.* 1 Corinthians 8:4–6)

## HOW WE USE ENGLISH DOES NOT DICTATE HOW HEBREWS USED HEBREW

The impulse to reject the divine council as henotheistic may be well-intentioned, but it amounts to trying to protect the Bible from itself by forcing it into modern religious categories and vocabulary that originate in the seventeenth century. It is a kind of false piety. We need to conform our thinking to Scripture, not vice versa; so we must accept that God himself is quite comfortable using the Hebrew word *elohim,* and the Greek word *theos*—"god"—to refer to beings other than himself. These didn't carry the theological baggage in Hebrew and Greek that "god" does in English; it was perfectly legitimate to call several different kinds of being an *elohim* or a *theos,* without suggesting that they were worthy of worship. Scripture strongly repudiates the idea that the gods of the divine council are anything like Yahweh; indeed, this is the point of expressions like Deuteronomy 4:35, which claims there is no god besides him—compare Zephaniah 2:15, where the same claim is made of cities besides Nineveh. The expression is obviously idiomatic: there is no god besides Yahweh in the sense that no god *compares* to him.[2]

## BICKERING OVER WORDS IS NOT THEOLOGICAL DEBATE

Debates are often swallowed up in pointless arguments about what terms mean. A common example I've had to deal with is atheists wanting to define atheism as a lack of belief in God, rather than as a belief in a lack of God.[3]

I don't really care *how* you define atheism. I care whether the view that there is no God is true. Similarly, I don't really care how you define divine council theology. I care whether the view the term describes is true.

The words monotheism and henotheism are not helpful here. They are not helpful for describing the nuances of theology we find in the Bible, precisely because they are synthetic Western Enlightenment categories made up centuries after Scripture was written to describe theoretical—and sometimes bogus—religious taxonomies. The authors and audiences of the Bible did not think about the spiritual realm in these ways. What we should be doing, instead of sticking labels to people's backs, is marking out the *actual views* in question. Here are three basic distinctions to draw when it comes to discussing divine council theology:

1. The English term *god*, with its commensurate adjective *divine*, is only broadly equivalent to the Hebrew term

---

2. For more, see Michael S. Heiser, "Does Divine Plurality in the Hebrew Bible Demonstrate an Evolution From Polytheism to Monotheism in Israelite Religion?" *JESOT* 1.1 (2012): http://jesot.org/wp-content/uploads/2012/04/JESOT-1.1-Heiser.pdf.

3. This is just an example, unrelated to the topic of the divine council, so I won't explicate it here, but see Bill Vallicella, "Against Terminological Mischief: 'Negative Atheism' and 'Negative Nominalism'" on Maverick Philosopher (March 2009): https://maverickphilosopher.typepad.com/maverick_philosopher/2009/03/against-terminological-mischief-negative-atheism-and-negative-nominalism.html.

*elohim*. Following Heiser, I would argue that *elohim* refers to residence and role, rather than to ontology:

> There are at least five (and I would argue for six) things that are called אלהים in the Hebrew Bible.
>
> A. Yahweh, the God of Israel (over 2000 times)
>
> B. The אלהים of Yahweh's heavenly council, both loyal and disloyal (Psa 82; Psa 89; *cf.* Deut 32:8–9, 43 [with LXX, Qumran5]; Psa 58:11)
>
> C. The gods of foreign nations (*e.g.*, 1 Kings 11:33)
>
> D. "Demons" (שדים; Deut 32:17)
>
> E. The disembodied human dead (1 Sam 28:13)
>
> F. Angels (Gen 35:7—the context of the plural predicator with אלהים subject; I believe it ultimately refers back to the angel of Yahweh)
>
> This listing alone should inform biblical scholars of something critical to the discussion, but which seems to have gone unnoticed. The fact that the biblical writers could use אלהים of more than one entity or figure—all of which are elsewhere described in far lesser terms than Yahweh—tells us clearly that they did not associate the term אלהים with a specific set of attributes. We do that reflexively as moderns—we use "g-o-d" thinking of the singular Being we know as the God of the Bible. Consequently, we feel uncomfortable with other אלהים no matter how clear the biblical text is in that regard. The biblical writer did not think about אלהים the way we think of "g-o-d." They did not presume that אלהים spoke of specific attributes that might be shared equally between Yahweh and other entities called אלהים.[4]

---

4. Heiser, "Divine Plurality."

Thus, supposing the Bible teaches that other *elohim* exist, the claim is that spiritual beings with certain authority exist; nothing more. It's understandable to be uncomfortable about calling them gods, or referring to them as divine, given the traditional English usage of these words. But discomfort or tension between the Bible's usage and ours is not a legitimate excuse to avoid the Bible's usage! We should instead *become* comfortable using terms like "gods" and "divine beings," because it reflects the Bible's own language, and we have a duty to conform our language to God's—not vice versa. "Divine" is the adjective associated with the noun "god," which in turn is the word we use to translate the Hebrew *elohim*. Since the Bible explicitly refers to angels as *elohim* (Hebrews 2:7 quoting Psalm 8:5), and gives us clear examples of them in council with God (1 Kings 22:19–22), the charge that this entails something like polytheism or henotheism, from my perspective, just looks like fundamentalism rearing its ugly head: a reaction against the discomforting fact that the Bible uses language differently than our tradition does—with all that implies.

2. Whatever you call them, these gods are *created* beings. God is the sole *transcendent* being.

3. The divine council view explicitly denies that these beings are worthy of worship. Thus, at best, you could argue that the divine council view is *monolatrous*. But there's still the question of whether monolatry presupposes that all gods are in the same general ontological category. If so, that label fails to apply either, in view of (2) above. Whatever you think about the divine council view, it is unimpeachably biblical in its affirmation of God's transcendence and "ontological peerlessness." So just say that instead of trying to find a label.

## 2. 1 CORINTHIANS 8:4–6 DENIES THE EXISTENCE OF OTHER GODS

Evangelicals tend to favor the ESV, so for those in search of a quick win, I Corinthians 8:4–6 looks like a promising haven once the charge of polytheism or henotheism doesn't stick. This is as ironic as it is unfortunate, because the appeal demonstrates how strongly our use of language influences our theology—and how strongly our theology influences our use of language:

> Therefore, as to the eating of food offered to idols, we know that "an idol has no real existence," and that "there is no God but one." For although there may be so-called gods in heaven or on earth—as indeed there are many "gods" and many "lords"—yet for us there is one God, the Father, from whom are all things and for whom we exist, and one Lord, Jesus Christ, through whom are all things and through whom we exist. (I Corinthians 4:8–6, ESV)

The unfortunate irony here is that **the Greek explicitly says that there *are* many gods and many lords.** The ESV takes the liberty of *interpreting* the text, rather than *translating* it. (In fairness, it is hardly alone here; most translations prejudge the meaning rather than letting the reader decide.)

What Paul actually wrote was not that there may be "*so*-called gods," but that there may be "*those* called gods." He also didn't use scare-quotes, because scare-quotes don't exist in Koine Greek.

Young does a good job here, but *cf.* NHEB, KJV, WEB, ASV, ISV and others:

> ...for even if there are those called gods, whether in heaven, whether upon earth—as there are gods many and lords many—yet to us is one God, the Father, of whom are the all things, and we to Him; and one Lord,

> Jesus Christ, through whom are the all things, and we
> through Him... (1 Corinthians 8:5–6, YLT)

By the same token, verse 4 does not say an idol has "no existence" as the ESV would have it; it says an idol is "nothing in the world." Whether or not Paul is quoting the Corinthians here (he certainly may be), it cannot be that an idol has *no* existence, since that is a contradiction in terms; but neither can it be that the deity it *represents* has no existence, since otherwise Paul contradicts himself in chapter 10:

> Therefore, what am I saying? That food sacrificed to idols is anything, or that an idol is anything? No, but that the things which they sacrifice, they sacrifice to demons and not to God, and I do not want you to become sharers with demons. (1 Corinthians 10:19–20, ESV)

Paul here echoes his language from chapter 8, affirming that idols are indeed nothing—not because the powers they represent are nonexistent, but rather presumably because:

## I. IDOLS DON'T WORK

Simply put, they are not inhabited by or conterminous with deities, as their users suppose. Sympathetic representation, the concept that makes idolatry sensible—*i.e.*, that by depicting a thing you come to participate in its nature—is false. While idolaters may have believed that the god became in some way joined to the idol through the principle of identification, this belief traded on a monistic understanding of creation where representation had causal power—which it does not. (Things actually work the other way around: we are identified with Jesus, for instance, because we are joined to him.) Moreover, there's no particular reason to think that *most* gods are real; the Bible is clear that there are gods who rule over nations, but the picture of the spiritual realm depicted in Acts 17:16, 23, where there was a god for literally every contingency, is certainly nonsense. This is why passages like Jeremiah 10:8–9 can describe idols as vanities and mere blocks of wood—the idols themselves really *were* nothing (*cf.* Isaiah 44:14–20)—yet verse 11 simultaneously presupposes the *existence* of other gods:

> They are both stupid and foolish;
> the instruction of idols is but wood!
> Beaten silver is brought from Tarshish,
> and gold from Uphaz.
> They are the work of the craftsman and of the hands
> of the goldsmith;
> their clothing is violet and purple;
> they are all the work of skilled men.
> But Yahweh is the true God;
> he is the living God and the everlasting King.
> At his wrath the earth quakes,
> and the nations cannot endure his indignation.
> Thus shall you say to them: **"The gods who did not make the heavens and the earth shall perish** from the earth and from under the heavens." (Jeremiah 10:8–11)

## II. THE BEINGS BEHIND THEM ARE AS NOTHING COMPARED TO GOD

Clearly spiritual beings *do* stand behind idols, as Paul and Jeremiah straightforwardly say—but these beings might as well be nothing when compared with the power of Jesus. The comparison in 1 Corinthians 8 is clearly in terms of *importance*, as shown by the fact that Paul refers also to the *food* as nothing. It exists—but it doesn't matter. Again, putting the text beside Jeremiah

10 is a good starting point for drawing out this theology, but Paul is actually going back more directly to Deuteronomy 32:17, 22:

> They sacrificed to the demons, not God [*eloah*—singular], to gods [*elohim*—semantically plural] whom they had not known, new gods who came from recent times; their ancestors had not known them ... They annoyed me with what is not a god; they provoked me with their idols.

Here Moses explicitly links what we translate as demons, Hebrew *shedim*, evil spirits which certainly exist,[5] with *elohim*. He says these beings *are* in fact *elohim*, gods, and that the Israelites sacrificed to them, instead of to God (distinguished with the singular *eloah*). This was a violation of both the *shema* (Deuteronomy 6:4), and the first commandment (Exodus 20:3). Indeed, these are precisely what Paul himself is drawing on in 1 Corinthians 8:6: "to *us* there is one God"—the *shema*—but this by no means denies the existence of other gods. The stricture not only makes more sense if they *do* exist, but is almost incoherent if they do not; far from denying their existence, both Paul and Moses presuppose it. What they are denying, like the rest of Scripture's authors, is the propriety of worshiping these gods— hence the ambivalent language: "they are gods but they aren't." This is exactly what we should expect given the broad semantic range and ambiguity of the terms *elohim* and *theos*; indeed, it reflects exactly the same con-

---

5. As in Psalm 106:37, this is perhaps a loan-word from Akkadian *shedu*, a territorial or guardian spirit. Heiser opines this quite confidently but provides no explicit evidence (Michael S. Heiser, "The Elohim: What (or Who) Are They?" on LogosTalk (October 2017): https://blog.logos.com/2017/10/the-elohim-what-or-who-are-they/). Fred L. Horton, Jr., writing for the Holman Bible Dictionary, does the same ("Exorcism" in *Holman Bible Dictionary:* https://www.studylight.org/dictionaries/hbd/e/exorcism.html). In this they are perhaps following DDD, which itself provides no further justification ("Demon" in *Dictionary of Deities & Demons in the Bible,* Second Edition, eds. Karen Van Der Toorn et al (Wm. B. Eerdmans, 1999), 237).

cern that opponents of the divine council are voicing about applying the term *god* to other beings!

If Moses and Paul didn't think there were rulers in the heavenly places, gods over the nations, then they wouldn't say such things in places like Exodus 12:12; 1 Corinthians 2:8; 2 Corinthians 4:4; Ephesians 3:10; 6:12. And that is the real problem with appeals from divine council opponents. They pit Scripture against itself.

### 3. PSALM 82 IS SPEAKING OF HUMAN RULERS

Perhaps because Psalm 82 is such a useful nexus for understanding the divine council in the redemptive history of God's kingdom, it tends to be the passage most strongly attacked. The argument is simply that the *elohim* here are actually human judges or kings, metaphorically called gods, or given this title as some kind of appellative or honorific.

The most significant problem with this approach is not actually exegetical—though there are certainly problems there. Rather, it is the unstated assumption that if Psalm 82 is speaking of human rulers then the entire concept of the divine council unravels, along with its place in the narrative of God's kingdom.

But this is obviously absurd. You can't refute an expansive stream of biblical theology by doing a word study on one passage that feeds it. Neither the case for believing in spiritual rulers in the heavenly places, nor the case for their redemptive-historical trajectory, rides on Psalm 82. If this psalm were removed from the canon, nothing significant would change. We could still easily prove the divine council in Scripture, and we could still certainly piece together its redemptive-historical arc. That should be obvious given how little I use Psalm 82 in making my own case in the preceding chapters! It is certainly an excellent showpiece, because of how it ties the various threads together so neatly. But if it had never been written, that would put only a small dent in the rhetorical aesthetics of this book, and almost no dent at all in its factual basis.

That said, it's helpful to be prepared, so I will below give the general form of this objection, and then suggest a number of ways to respond. Here is how one Reformed correspondent put it to me:

> These verses (and remember they are poetry) must be and are saying: "You men have been exercising God-like functions—judging and ruling, you think of yourselves as gods, and I agree that you are behaving as though you were gods, but 'like men you shall die, and fall like any prince.'" This alone makes sense of the passage.

## "LIKE GODS" OR JUST GODS?

The first thing to note is the weaseling away from what the text actually says. This is not exegesis, which starts by analyzing the actual words; it is eisegesis, in which a pre-prepared interpretive gloss is quickly applied over the top of the actual words, to sanitize and neutralize them.

God does not merely agree that these rulers are *behaving like* gods; he declares that they *are* gods—and not merely gods, but sons:

> I, I have said you are gods, and sons of the Most High
> all of you (v. 6).

Could this mean that Yahweh has assigned them the appellatives "gods" and "sons" owing to their ruling in his stead? Possibly. Could it mean that he is merely agreeing that they are *acting* like gods and sons? That is exceedingly awkward. Certainly neither interpretation is self-evident; quite the opposite. To make this case, divine council opponents have to actually *argue*; and to do that, they must shoulder a huge burden of proof:

*i. They must show that the council of verse 1 is a council of men*

But the Hebrew *adat el* is a known cognate of the Ugaritic phrase *'dt 'ilm*, which was the term used in Canaan of the congregation of the gods; not of human rulers. Perhaps Psalm 82 is seeking to correct this usage, but if so, we should find clear evidence in the rest of the psalm to overturn their identification as divine beings and present them instead as human rulers—which we do not.

Moreover, a council of men is baffling on its own terms. Who are these men, and where are they located, such that God is standing in their midst? This is explicitly an *international* council; "all the foundations of the *eretz*" are shaken by their terrible rulership. Although *eretz* can just mean "land," in this case it is paralleled with the nations:

> Rise up, O God, judge the **earth**
> Because you shall inherit all the **nations.** (v. 8)

There can be no doubt, therefore, that this is an international council. But such a thing does not even exist today in the way described, let alone during the time of Israel! If it's a poetic device, it is an opaque one without parallel in Jewish thought. By contrast, a council of divine beings who ruled the nations is attested repeatedly in both Jewish and wider religious texts. So this attempted explanation is like suggesting that a news report about the president speaking from the White

House isn't referring to Donald Trump speaking from his residence in D.C., but to another unknown, possibly metaphorical president speaking from an unknown, possibly poetic house that also happens to be white.

*ii. They must show Scripture using the terms elohim and beney elohim to refer to men*

But *is* there anywhere in the Hebrew Bible—or the wider contemporary literature—where this is the case?

*Elohim* never refers to men. It always refers to spiritual beings; that is, in fact, the very thing that circumscribes its semantic range![6] Divine council opponents will sometimes appeal to Exodus 21:6; 22:8, but there is no compelling reason to translate *elohim* as semantically plural in these instances. "God" is the simplest reading, and indeed the only obvious one—aside from a circular requirement to find precedent for Psalm 82. The consistent usage of the Hebrew Bible is that *elohim* refers (exclusively, and with some diversity) to residents of the spirit world; never to living human beings.

The plural *beney elohim*, "sons of God" and its variations, is a term of art in Scripture, also never used of human beings. True—people are sometimes called God's sons (*e.g.*, 2 Samuel 7:14), but the specific plural wording, *beney elohim*, is not used on those occasions—precisely because it was a term of art, a religious meme referring to the divine council. Some would argue that it is used of human spirits in Job 1 and 2, but even if we grant that in the teeth of the evidence already adduced in this book, that interpretation runs aground when it hits Psalm 82. Consider the implications:

6. Heiser, "Divine Plurality."

1. **Deceased human spirits are rulers over the nations from heaven.** This is an awkward position for someone to take while simultaneously objecting to angelic spirits being rulers over the nations from heaven!

2. **Deceased human spirits judge wickedly from heaven.** Needless to say, this is incoherent on any orthodox soteriology—humans in heaven do not sin, because they are like God (1 John 3:2 etc). You cannot enter heaven, but then lose it again.

3. **Deceased human spirits are sentenced to die.** This is again embarrassing nonsense. How can God say, "you will die like men" when they have *already* died? And if this is the second death, how can they be subject to it as his redeemed people in heaven?

*iii. They must make sense of Jesus' appeal to Psalm 82 in John 10:34–39*

Seeing the losing case for a word studies approach here, divine council opponents will typically try to short-circuit the exegetical problems by appealing to Jesus' own interpretation of Psalm 82 in John 10. But this fumbles the clear reading of what Jesus, and his audience, actually think:

> The Jews picked up stones again to stone him. Jesus answered them, "I have shown you many good works from the Father; for which of them are you going to stone me?" The Jews answered him, "It is not for a good work that we are going to stone you but for blasphemy, because you, being a man, make yourself God."
> Jesus answered them, "Is it not written in your Law, 'I said, you are gods'? If he called them gods to whom the word of God came—and Scripture cannot be broken—do you say of him whom the Father con-

> secrated and sent into the world, 'You are blaspheming,' because I said, 'I am the Son of God'? If I am not doing the works of my Father, then do not believe me; but if I do them, even though you do not believe me, believe the works, that you may know and understand that the Father is in me and I am in the Father."
>
> Again they sought to arrest him, but he escaped from their hands. (John 10:31–39)

Jesus' argument here is an a fortiori one—probably his favorite form of inference. If we lay it out syllogistically, it would look roughly like this:

1. God himself calls lesser divine beings gods and makes them adoptive sons of the Most High (Psalm 82:6);
2. Jesus is not merely an adopted son; he is in the Father, and the Father is in him (John 10:38);
3. Therefore, how much more a son and how much more equal with God is he.

On the other hand, if you take the word of God to have come to human beings in Psalm 82, then the argument runs aground:

4. God himself calls human rulers gods and makes them adoptive sons of the Most High (Psalm 82:6);
5. Jesus is not merely an adopted son; he is in the Father, and the Father is in him (John 10:38);
6. Therefore, how much more a son and how much more equal with God is he.

The problem here is that the connection between (4) to (5) is fatally equivocal. Under this interpretation, the term "gods" is honorific; it is an appellative that doesn't denote a divine role or non-human ontology. But the Jews' outrage is prompted precisely because the claims Jesus is making *are* about role and ontology. This interpretation has him justifying his claim to divinity on the basis of an honorific title that can be applied to any man—which is an obvious non sequitur.

The fact that the Jews again seek to stone him after hearing this argument is ample demonstration that they did not interpret Psalm 82 as referring to human beings, nor Jesus as saying, in effect, "Cool it guys, we're all gods here." Rather, they see him as doubling down on what they suppose is blasphemy. The repeated emphasis in John is on Jesus' divinity as the Word of God, so we should expect Jesus to amplify, rather than downplay or backpedal, his claim to divinity. Which is more likely in view of Jesus' mission and John's theological focus: that we should understand him to be *emptying* the term gods of so much import that it can be applied even to his unbelieving audience—or *using* its import to expand and justify his own claim to godhood? The former is obviously 180 degrees from what we should expect. It is unsurprising, then, that the human interpretation makes no sense of Jesus' argument, nor his opponents' response.

*iv. They must make sense of men dying like men*

A final rejoinder at this point, as the lines of argument run dry, is that gods cannot die—so even if the human council interpretation of Psalm 82 is poor, the divine council alternative is incoherent in light of verse 7:

> However, you will die like man [or men],
> and you will fall like one of the princes.

I think this objection arises only on the spur of the moment, because if you take the time to think it through, it actually obliterates the human council interpretation. Consider: God says that, despite his declaring these beings to be gods, they will nonetheless die like man and fall like any prince. This contrast only works if there *is* a contrast; *i.e.*, if these gods are *greater* than the typical prince, and if it is *unnatural* for them to die like man. What possible sense does it make to tell men that they will die like men, or princes that they will fall like princes? Such an interpretation turns the psalmist into a rhetorical dunce with no competence in his craft.

While men dying like men makes no sense at all, gods dying like men certainly does. Confusion only arises if we ignore the theology of death articulated in Scripture, and think of it in purely biological terms. But in the Bible, death is not primarily a *biological* event; it is a *relational* one. Biology is incidental: death itself is separation from God's benevolence, and exposure to his wrath. The very first time we see death, in Genesis 2:16–17, God solemnly promises it to Adam and Eve should they eat from the tree. He neither lied nor changed his mind—they *did* die on the day they ate, as presupposed by Paul in Ephesians 2:1; Colossians 2:13 etc. Death simply isn't biological at root.

The first death was in Eden; the second death is in the lake of fire (Revelation 21:8). *Neither* of these is biological. To the contrary, the second death involves eternal biological *life.*

Now, here's the kicker: Jesus in Matthew 25:41 explicitly states that this lake of fire, this second *death*, is prepared for the devil and his angels—some of whom are the very beings addressed in Psalm 82. If the lake of fire is explicitly described as (i) death, and (ii) originally for wicked spiritual beings, then the judgment of Psalm 82 makes explicit sense when applied to wicked spiritual beings!

So Psalm 82:7 does not require us think that biological death is in view; rather, it is establishing a contrast between these gods' status (v. 6) and their punishment (v. 7). The parallelism emphasizes that their fate will be the same as that of men. It is an ironic reversal—indeed, an allusion to the original ironic reversal in Genesis 3:14–15. By failing to fulfill the role of divinity, these beings are made lower than the men they were supposed to rule. Just as Satan does not eat literal dust in Genesis 3:14, and just as he is not brought down into a literal pit in Isaiah 14:15, so these gods are not literally killed in Psalm 82:6–7. The point is much like that in Isaiah 14—indeed, the language of "falling" is even the same:

> **How you have fallen from heaven,** O morning star, son of dawn!
> You are cut down to the ground, conqueror of nations!
> And you said in your heart,
> "I will ascend to heaven;
> I will raise up my throne above the stars of God;
> and I will sit on the mountain of assembly
> on the summit of Tsaphon;
> I will ascend to the high places of the clouds,
> I will make myself like the Most High."
> **But you are brought down to Sheol,**
> to the far reaches of the pit. (Isaiah 14:12–15)

To be brought down to Sheol, of course, is to be brought down to the grave, to the underworld. It is a metaphor for biological death when applied to human beings. Yet we do not think that Isaiah is therefore teaching that Satan dies in that sense; nor do we suppose the passage can only be speaking of a human king, and *not* of Satan. For the same reason, it strains Psalm 82:7 to take the judgment of death as strictly biological. It is referring, rather, to the gods faring no better than human rulers who are weak and mortal, who cannot rule forever.

## 4. WHY THINK THE RULERS OF 1 CORINTHIANS 2:6–8 ARE GODS?

This is not necessarily an objection, per se, but it is a question worth addressing here for the sake of completeness, and so you can present a well-rounded case. Here's 1 Corinthians 2:1–9:

> And I, when I came to you, brothers, did not come with superiority of speech or of wisdom, proclaiming to you the testimony of God. For I decided not to know anything among you except Jesus Anointed and him crucified. And I came to you in weakness and in fear and with much trembling, and my speech and my preaching were not with the persuasiveness of wisdom, but with a demonstration of the Spirit and power, in order that your faith would not be in the wisdom of men, but in the power of God. Now we do speak wisdom among the mature, but wisdom not of this age or of the rulers of this age, who are perishing, but we speak the hidden wisdom of God, a revealed truth, which God predestined before the ages for our glory, which none of the rulers of this age knew. For if they had known it, they would not have crucified the Lord of glory.

This is the discussion in which these rulers appear: a discussion of God's wisdom unto salvation, hidden from the rulers of this age, but now revealed through the Spirit. There are two related reasons to think the rulers are (primarily) spiritual:

### I. THEY ARE OF "THIS AGE"

Comparing how the phrase "this age" is used elsewhere suggests sinister spiritual overtones. It refers to the world, but especially to the world as a dominion; this is clear in Romans 12:2. Earlier in 1 Corinthians, Paul even parallels it with *kosmos* (1 Corinthians 1:20; *cf.* John 12:31). But while this by no means excludes human rulers, it surely must encompass *more* than them, for a couple of reasons:

1. The human rulers of the *world* did not crucify Jesus; the human rulers of *Israel* did, both Roman and Jewish. One could reply that Paul is using a synecdoche to illustrate that these rulers represented the opposition of the whole dominion of man to God. And I am indeed sympathetic to this argument, not least of all because it *strengthens* the point that it was spiritual rulers as much as human ones behind the crucifixion; we know from places like Psalm 82 and John 12:31 that the ultimate rulers of the world are spiritual beings. So if this is a synecdoche, then the rulers Paul has in mind here are first spiritual, and then subordinately human. Both being in view seems to be corroborated by verse 9's "heart of man"—suggesting human rulers on Paul's mind—and verse 12's "spirit of this world"—suggesting Satan on his mind.

2. To build on this point, when Paul uses the term "this age" he sets up an implicit contrast with the age to come, ruled by Jesus (which is probably the age about to dawn in AD 70—though of course even now they are ruling in the sense of exercising power, so it's not entirely clear). He does the same in 2 Corinthians 4:4 and Galatians 1:4. His language is calculated to point to the rulers of the *entire* age and the *entire* world, rather than merely to human beings ruling a fraction of it for a fraction of time. The broad scope surely points to the same rulers that are on his mind in Ephesians 3:10, which has close conceptual parallels with 1 Corinthians 2:8. In Ephesians 3:8–11, the mystery (Gk. *musterion*, "re-

vealed truth") of the gospel is hidden for the ages from the rulers *in the heavenly places*, before being unveiled through the congregation. In 1 Corinthians 2:6–10, the mystery of the gospel is hidden for the ages from the rulers (location unspecified)—who, had they known it, would never have crucified Jesus—and is now revealed through the Spirit. The connection of ideas is too obvious to doubt that Paul is describing basically the same thing, *even if* he also has human rulers in view in 1 Corinthians 2, as appropriate to its context of human wisdom and power.

## I. WHAT ARE THE RULERS' MOTIVATIONS?

Had the rulers understood the wisdom imparted to the Corinthians—namely the hidden plan of God to redeem mankind through the cross—Paul says they would never have played a part in it. They would never have actually crucified Jesus. But why? There are two aspects to this: the negative and the positive. The negative is obvious; the positive less so.

*Negatively, human motives don't make sense of Paul's comment*

There's no clear reason that human rulers *wouldn't* have crucified Jesus if they had known God's plan. Much of the point of the Bible's language about the world as the dominion of man is how much it hates God and his representatives, and how much under God's judgment it therefore is (John 3:19; 15:18–19 etc). On two separate levels, it makes no sense to imagine that human rulers would have refrained from executing Jesus:

1.  The plan of redemption which the rulers did not know trades on Jesus' identity as Yahweh. The whole point of parables like that of the tenants is how the rulers of Israel *did* have some inkling of this (*cf.* Matthew 22:41–45); it was precisely because of their wicked pattern of killing God's messengers that they escalated to killing his own son (Matthew 21:38–39—although compare "inheritance" here and in Psalm 82:8; the divine council is implicitly working in the background). Is there any reason to think they would have submitted to Jesus had they more fully understood his identity? Given their antipathy toward God, is it not more likely that they would have killed him sooner? After all, much of their motivation was the threat he presented to their own authority—but a rival who is *actually the Anointed* is certainly *more* of a threat than a rival who just claims to be.

2.  It would, in a twisted kind of way, be in their best interests to crucify Jesus, with apologies, since that is what makes salvation possible for them! Certainly the rulers who authorized the crucifixion were not interested in salvation—at least at the time—but would they have *prevented* it, knowing that it was the satisfaction of God's wrath against sin? Given their hatred of Jesus, why not eat their cake and have it too—kill him, and let God's wrath fall on him as a backup plan?

*Positively, angelic motives make perfect sense of Paul's comment*

While human rulers would have killed Jesus anyway, the gods most certainly would not have. This is because it was the cross that was their undoing. They *thought* they were wrecking God's plan of establishing a human-ruled kingdom on earth; in fact they were abetting it. They *thought* they were wresting the world away from God; in fact they were giving it to him. Paul is plain in Colossians 2:15 that it was because of the cross that the "rulers and authorities" were disarmed and shamed. That statement comes in the context of the debt of sin against us (*viz.* Satan—"accuser"); it cannot be speaking of human rulers, but is rather making the same point as John 12:31 and 1 Peter 3:22: that the cross broke the power of the gods over men by putting a man over *them*.

This becomes extremely clear within the biblical theology of kingdom, if we simply follow the implications of Paul's thought sequence in 1 Corinthians 2. Here's how it works:

In verse 7, Paul explains that the gospel is a revealed truth, which God predestined before the ages for our glory—which, had the rulers of this age understood it, they would never have crucified the Lord of that glory. The point here is subtle because it is implicit, but Paul is referring to the glorification of believers that he discusses elsewhere:

> For all who are led by the Spirit of God are sons of God. For you did not receive the spirit of slavery to fall back into fear, but you have received the Spirit of adoption as sons, by whom we cry, "Abba! Father!" The Spirit himself bears witness with our spirit that we are children of God, and if children, then heirs—heirs of God and fellow heirs with Anointed, provided we suffer with him in order that we may also be glorified with him. (Romans 8:14–17)

There's nothing controversial or unexpected here; Christians all know that Jesus became like us so we could become like him. They might not put it that way, but anyone with a basic grasp of the faith knows that the final stage of salvation is glorification:

> For those whom he foreknew he also predestined to
> be conformed to the image of his Son, in order that
> he might be the firstborn among many brothers. And
> those whom he predestined he also called, and those
> whom he called he also justified, and those whom he
> justified he also glorified. (Romans 8:29–30)

As John puts it, Jesus has given his glory to us (John
17:22). So far, so good.

But what happens to the existing sons of God when
believers are finally glorified?

Do you not know that someday we will judge angels (1
Corinthians 6:2–3)? This is why Paul adds that he is so
certain that neither death nor life, nor *angels nor rulers,*
nor things present nor things to come, *nor powers* can
separate us from the love of God in Jesus. Their power to
accuse us is broken (Romans 8:33–34), and we will someday judge them. God is replacing the wicked sons of God
as the rulers of the nations, by establishing a human
king, and adopting a new family to rule with him (Revelation 2:26–27; 3:21).

All this happens *only* because Jesus satisfied God's
wrath against human sin on the cross, sanctified and
renewed the human nature by rising again, and restored a human king to Adam's kingdom by receiving
all dominion afterwards. The gods, in sending Jesus to
the cross, thought they were eliminating the rival to
their rule and seizing his inheritance (Matthew
21:38–39; *cf.* Psalm 82:8). In fact, they were raising him
up to receive that inheritance—and in so doing they
sealed their own promised judgment (Psalm 82:7). If
they had known *that* would happen, truly they would
*never* have crucified the Lord of glory!

# BAPTISM AS A PLEDGE OF ALLEGIANCE

*Baptism is (among other things) a public renouncement of one's former enslavement to Satan and the other spiritual rulers of this present darkness, and a vow of fealty to the enthroned king, Jesus.*

## KOOK NOTE

Before we begin I have to break out my Kook Hat again and explain that, although I have just used the word baptism twice for the sake of clarity, I shan't do it in the body of this appendix except with theological terms of art. This is because there is no sound reason to *transliterate* the *baptizo* word group, rather than to *translate* from the Greek as we would with any other words. The translator's job is to render the *meaning* of words from one language into another, not to simply take the *sounds* from one and convert them into the other. Transliteration of this sort does the very opposite of what a translator should be aiming for: it turns the transliterated word into jargon, the meaning of which becomes dependent on the reader's understanding of this jargon, rather than on the meaning of the term in the original language.[1] (The exception to this rule is names; these *should* be transliterated since it is their *sounds* that function as tokens of identification, even when the meanings of these sounds are also of crucial value and should be footnoted. Hence my issue with "the LORD" in place of Yahweh.)

The transliteration problem is nowhere more apparent than in the English term *baptism*, which is an item of religious jargon that actually obscures the meaning of, and connections within, the text of Scripture. It is Christianese. If you doubt this, simply take a moment to translate *every* word in the Great Commission, and see if you notice a difference. Like most Greek words, *baptizo* can be translated different ways depending on its context; it typically means to immerse, but sometimes a better rendering is to submerge or to wash or even to overwhelm.[2] There is no single English word with a similar semantic range, but the key point is that *baptizo* was not a technical term for a sacrament in Greek; it was an ordinary term used of things like cloths being dyed, ships being sunk, and people being bathed. Hence I shall translate it as such.

---

Although the implications for the sacrament are probably obvious, I don't mean to stake out a position on this here. If you're not much of an immerser, I'll throw you a bone and note that the "baptism" of the Spirit is linked to *ekcheo*, "pouring," in *e.g.* Acts 2:17–18. But I'm quite content with the level of controversy this book is operating at already, without twisting *that* dial any further.

---

1. For an excellent discussion that makes my case much more fully, see Benjamin J. Snyder, "Technical Term or Technical Foul? βαπτίζω (Baptizō) and the Problem of Transliteration as Translation" (October 2018): https://www.researchgate.net/publication/328108514_Technical_Term_or_Technical_Foul_baptizo_Baptizo_and_the_Problem_of_Transliteration_as_Translation.

2. *E.g.*, Fred Karlson, "What Is the Primary Meaning of Baptism? Some Translational Difficulties" on Bible.org (March 2006): https://bible.org/article/what-primary-meaning-baptism-some-translational-difficulties.

## SO LET'S TALK ABOUT IMMERSION

With that covered, let's consider a neglected biblical-theological angle on New Testament immersion, and how it connects back to the gospel of the kingdom. We'll start with Mark 16:16, which is a classically troubling text to many Christians who recognize the errors of either baptismal regeneration or works-righteousness:

> Whoever believes **and is immersed** will be saved, but whoever does not believe will be condemned. (Mark 16:16)

It doesn't do much good to argue that this is probably not original to Mark, because the sentiment is echoed elsewhere, as we'll see shortly. So how should we understand it? Is immersion required for salvation?

There are several things we could say about the logic of Mark 16:16, but what I want to focus on is the rhetorical structure. The verse is a kind of antithetical parallelism—a figure of speech in which two similar but opposing ideas are contrasted. Parallelisms trade on symmetry: what is true of the first part must also be true of the second (in this case, in reverse).

The reason I bring this up is that there is an apparent *asymmetry* here: the first part mentions both belief and immersion; the second part mentions only belief. But since what is true of the second part must be true of the first—only in reverse—the rhetorical effect is such that belief-and-immersion in the first means the same thing as just belief in the second. Jesus does not say that whoever does not believe *and is not immersed* will be condemned; he says only that those who do not believe will be. Given the structure of the parallel, he is speaking about the *same thing* in the second part as in the first; it therefore follows that immersion must be a kind of merism that describes what it means to believe.

But how can that be? In what way does immersion describe belief? How can it be considered somehow synonymous with believing?

## FAITH AS ALLEGIANCE

This is easy to answer within the context of kingdom theology—but doing so has implications. Just as kingdom theology challenges the emaciated evangelical gospel, reframing the demands of that gospel challenges the emaciated evangelical understanding of *sola fide*:

> The Greek term *pistis*, which is usually translated as belief or faith, doesn't typically mean mere intellectual agreement. Rather, it often refers to allegiance or fealty toward a king.

For example, in 3 Maccabees 3:2 (NRSV) the Jews are said to continue to "maintain goodwill and unswerving loyalty [*pistis*] toward the dynasty." In a similar statement in 5:31, Ptolemy notes that they have showed "a full and firm loyalty [*pistis*]" to his ancestors. The Greek expansions to Esther 3 similarly describes Haman's relationship to King Artaxerxes as one of "unchanging goodwill and steadfast fidelity [*pistis*]" while Josephus, writing c. AD 75, uses *pistis* routinely to refer to allegiance or loyalty (some examples are: *Antiquities* 12.47, 147, 396; *The Jewish War* 1.207; 2.341).[3]

---

3. Cited in Matthew W. Bates, *Salvation by Allegiance Alone: Rethinking Faith, Works, and the Gospel of Jesus the King* (Baker Academic, 2017).

So if *pistis* is as much about allegiance as it is about belief, Mark's identifying immersion with *pistis* suggests that being immersed is a paradigm case of showing allegiance; a token that stands in place of *pistis* itself.[4] Although this sounds odd to our ears, it is a typically Jewish way of thinking—in terms of wholes rather than their parts, and in terms of combining rather than dividing or categorizing. It's called **Semitic Totality.**[5]

This suggests that Mark sees immersion as a kind of *pledge of allegiance.* I think this is corroborated quite explicitly by 1 Peter 3:21—another classically troubling text for Protestants. Peter sees immersion precisely in these terms. If this is right, the parallelism of Mark 16:16 is saying, in effect, that:

> Whoever places allegiance and pledges allegiance will be saved, but whoever does not place allegiance will be condemned.

## IMMERSION AS A PLEDGE OF ALLEGIANCE IN 1 PETER

So why do I think that Peter imagines immersion as a pledge of allegiance? Here's the text:

> Immersion, which corresponds to this, now saves you, not as a removal of dirt from the body but as a pledge [*eperotema*] to God of a good conscience [*syneidesis*], through the resurrection of Jesus Anointed. (1 Peter 3:21)

---

4. For a different angle on the same idea, see D. Bnonn Tennant, "Does James teach justification by works?" (March 2015): https://bnonn.com/does-james-teach-justification-by-works/, in which I challenge the common Reformed view that "justification" in 2:20–4 is speaking of something other than credited righteousness, and demonstrate how faith is "worky" in the view of both James and Paul.

5. *E.g.*, Bernard J. LeFrois, "Semitic Totality Thinking," *The Catholic Biblical Quarterly* (1955), 17, no. 2:195–03: http://www.jstor.org/stable/43710136.

BDAG and others note that *eperotema* can mean both pledge and appeal. This is reflected in the divided translation choices that different Bibles make: the NIV, NET, HCSB and others say pledge; the ESV, NASB, NHEB and others say appeal; the BLB even says demand. Others try to hedge their bets in various ways; Faithlife's LEB translates it appeal, but in the study notes it adds, "a pledge of loyalty to God;" the NLT preserves the ambiguity by rendering *eperotema* as response.

I think surely this last choice is basically right, in that it recognizes both ways as valid: Peter is using a double entendre. This is a pledge of the kind of allegiance that appeals to God's mercy.

By the same token, *syneidesis* ("a good conscience") refers at least as much to attentiveness to obligation as mere moral knowledge (*cf.* 1 Timothy 1:5; 1 Corinthians 10:25, 27-29; Hebrews 9:9, 14). *I.e.*, it is not just a moral compass that "points us north," toward God; rather, it is our particular effort of *going* north, toward God; of *heeding* the needle's pull. Peter isn't merely saying that we *appeal* to God *for* a clear conscience in immersion. He is saying that we *pledge* fealty to God *from/with/out of* a clear conscience (*cf.* Hebrews 10:22–23).

Translating verse 21 this way also makes much more sense of 1 Peter 3:22, which emphasizes Jesus' kingship over all things. The thought-sequence is consistent: immersion saves us as a pledge of allegiance, made to the king out of a clear conscience, relying on the resurrection as the power and proof of our adoption into his family (*cf.* 1 Peter 1:3).

## OTHER STRANDS OF EVIDENCE

Romans 6:3–4 further links immersion to an identification with Jesus' death and resurrection, by which we publicly declare our union and participation with him *in toto* (vv. 5–14; *cf.* Galatians 2:20). There is an analogy between Jesus being raised from death, and our being raised from the water. Since the resurrection was how God publicly testified that Jesus was his now-reigning king (Romans 1:4), immersion is, by analogy, how *we* testify that Jesus is *our* now-reigning king, and that we are seated with him in the heavenly places (Ephesians 2:6). In the same way, Ephesians 5:26 suggests by analogy that immersion is how we are publicly set apart to God ("sanctified").

Moreover, Christian immersion has its roots in John's immersion, which was a public profession of repentance (Matthew 3:6; Acts 13:24 etc). This is why Peter tells the Jews to repent and be immersed—it is a parallelism that required no further explanation, because they already understood that to be immersed just *was* to publicly repent: to turn from one's loyalty to self and sin and other gods (*cf.* Psalm 82:1; Exodus 12:12; 1 Corinthians 8:5 etc), and to pledge allegiance to Jesus. Now, obviously there was a qualitative difference between the immersions of John and Jesus, which is why the latter was necessary—but the point is that immersion itself as a public profession of faithfulness was taken for granted (*cf.* Acts 16:15).

This view of immersion as a pledge is also reflected in the early church. Tertullian, writing early in the third century, observes:

> When we are going to enter the water, but a little before, in the presence of the congregation and under the hand of the president, we solemnly profess that **we disown the devil, and his pomp, and his angels.** Hereupon we are thrice immersed, making a some-

what ampler **pledge** than the Lord has appointed in the Gospel.[6]

Interestingly, Tertullian elsewhere refers to immersion as "the solemn declaration of the sacrament"[7]—and the Latin word *sacramentum* itself originally referred to a pledge or oath; as, for instance, a Roman soldier's oath of allegiance to the emperor.

Obviously there is more we could say here, but the takeaway is that immersion is a public renouncement of one's former enslavement to Satan and the other spiritual rulers of this present darkness (Ephesians 6:12 etc), and a pledge of allegiance to the enthroned king, Jesus.

6. Tertullian, *Of the Soldier's Crown*, 3. This profession is still used today, especially in high church traditions.

7. *Idem.*, 14.

www.ingramcontent.com/pod-product-compliance
Lightning Source LLC
Chambersburg PA
CBHW032025050726

47590CB00006B/2304